The Complete Works of
François Villon

THE COMPLETE WORKS OF
FRANÇOIS VILLON

Translated
with a biography and notes by
ANTHONY BONNER

With an introduction by
WILLIAM CARLOS WILLIAMS

DAVID McKAY COMPANY, INC.
NEW YORK

Item, et a mon plus que maistre,
L. B.

CONTENTS

INTRODUCTION

by WILLIAM CARLOS WILLIAMS

By a single line of verse in an almost forgotten language, Medieval French, the name of Villon goes on living defiantly; our efforts, as we seem to try to efface it, polish and make it shine the more. What is that secret that has escaped with a mere question, deftly phrased, the profundity of the ages:

> Mais ou sont les neiges d'antan?

All that has been forgotten (or, better said, all that would gladly have been forgotten) by the poet Villon in his fifteenth-century France has remained so vividly alive, present in everything we are, that it lives on in answer to that eternal question.

There are no more than three thousand lines to the whole body of his verse, but they keep an intensity of consciousness about them that is not contrived. There is no invention about them. They are a recital about the man's life with the simple question that he permits himself in retrospect.

It is a recital of a tough life as a student of the arts about Paris. His father had died when he was a boy. They were poor. His mother whom he loved by evidence of one of his most poignant ballades must have kept pace with him during his student years; but rid of his father he was faced from the beginning with disaster and thrown on the town, a princely Paris, which, with his imagination raging among the rude splendors of those times, he was obliged to witness right at his back door—with an empty pocket.

A student, like all intelligent and high-spirited students,

he must have been inclined to kick over the traces. But without the overt, insistent churchly insistences of his mother he must have wandered the city's shabbier dives whenever he felt the urge to go wherever the fancy took him. But his art, bred of his literary training, was a restraining influence that protected him. A scholar, schooled in the university, hard-headed and protected by a conservatism nothing could move, he had been reared in a tradition of scholarship which kept his head high—nothing could rob him of that pride.

A thief who had killed his man, though his life had been threatened equally, he had had to bear the early stigma of that accusation. No one could have been there to shield him; he was not ducking out. Poor, as he confessed he was in *The Legacy*, he had nowhere to go but to his attic room where the ink froze in his inkwell. Rather than yield to the bitter pressure of the circumstances he had to write to keep himself warm; his mind required it.

The striking thing is that, as with all such men, he never let a thought enter his head of smudging the surface of his art. The great Cézanne or Van Gogh and many lesser men have been the same—born fools as far as the pristine virtues of their inspiration are concerned.

But Villon was a poet strictly trained in his measures. He could not change the poet's meticulous training, or his view of the world that surrounded him, without giving up the whole game. He must have persisted in it, since everything else had been early lost. He was fixed in his conception of his task; he must, having found a release in his desperation, persist in a certain mode without varying—persist to the end. It was all he knew. His eager mind presented with its problem—the writing of a certain cast of verse, the ballade and the eight line stanzas of *The Testament*—did not know better than to repeat the pattern over and over, since he could not escape and retain his integrity.

So that his mind was beating about into all crevices of his being—while his invention, anchored in the technique of his craft, was stilled. It was a fixed form, fortunately for him, in which his invention could be released. There it could not contain itself: the minute dilemmas of his words in finding the exact niche for themselves into which they must have fitted to satisfy his spirit. Invention? What the hell are you going to invent, he is certain to have said. The facts are there, properly named if a man has the courage to use them with art enough; and I have the courage and the art—and time to use it.

He was a curiously factual person. A fact is a fact and a name is a name however you or the liars about you seek to hide it. It can be marshalled as in a poem, drilled until it falls into its proper place in the line, but you cannot escape it. Is it not the truth? Everything else is an escape from the truth and by my mother's memory there is nothing sacred but the truth.

"As far as art or the technical part of poetry goes, . . ."* (Then begins a statement typical of some critics, especially some British, who allow their disapproval of the uncompromising candor of Villon's statements to influence their judgments of the man's literary honesty.) ". . . in this way he was no better than, say, his patron, Charles d'Orléans." (True enough, I presume, but as subtle an understatement as could be conceived. The true situation, as far as the *poet* Villon is concerned, is that Charles d'Orléans cannot even be said to exist.)

(The logical figure must now be resolved with the same suavity with which it began; well written, I must say!) "Villon's *The Legacy* and *The Testament* are made up of eight-line stanzas of eight-syllabled verses, varied in the case of *The Testament* by the insertion of ballades and rondeaux of very great beauty and interest, but not formally different in any way from poems of the same kind for more than a century past. What really distinguishes Villon is the intenser quality of his poetical feeling and expression, and what is perhaps arrogantly called the modern character of his subjects and thought. Medieval poetry, with rare exceptions, and, with exceptions not quite so rare, classical poetry, are distinguished by their lack of what is now called the personal note. In Villon this note sounds, struck with singular force and skill. Again, the simple joy of living which distinguishes both periods—the medieval, despite a common opinion, scarcely less than the ancient—has disappeared. Even the riot and rollicking of his earlier days are mentioned with far less relish of remembrance than sense of their vanity. This sense of vanity,

* Quoted passages by courtesy of the Encyclopaedia Britannica.

indeed, not of the merely religious, but of the purely mundane and even half-pagan kind, is Villon's most prominent characteristic. It tinges his narrative, despite its burlesque bequests, all through; it is the very keynote of his most famous and beautiful piece, the *Ballade des dames du temps jadis,* with its refrain, 'Mais ou sont les neiges d'antan?' as well as of his most daring piece of realism, the other ballade of *La Grosse Margot,* with its burden of hopeless entanglement in shameless vice. It is nowhere more clearly sounded than in the piece which ranks with these two at the head of his work, the *Regrets de la Belle Hëaulmiere,* in which a woman, once young and beautiful, now old and withered, laments her lost charms. So it is almost throughout his poems, including the grim *Epitaphe,* and hardly excluding the very beautiful *Ballade pour prier Nostre Dame,* with its description of sincere and humble piety. It is in the profound melancholy which the dominance of this note has thrown over Villon's work, and in the suitableness of that melancholy to the temper of all generations since, that his charm and power have consisted, though it is difficult to conceive any time at which his poetical merit could be ignored."

The man, a young man when he first became known to posterity, must have had a premonition of death from his earliest years which affected him not at all. What is so noteworthy about death that we are called on to give it any heed? But the art of making a distinguished poem is something else again.

He was intensely concerned with his art, but lost all interest after he had made use of it. That protected him from being, in the slightest way, the self-conscious maker of a mode of composition. He *was* his art and could not be separated from it. His poem by an extension of all its perquisites was himself. He lived in his accounts of even his own mother whom he celebrated in one of the least sentimental ballades. He saw her there before him and so she lives indestructibly.

The singular poem known as *The Legacy* contains his will, knowing he was a candidate for death from the first! This is a very early work written nonchalantly when he was twenty-five. It is perfect Villon. As a document it may not be as valuable as the later and more detailed and more virulent comment on his times *The Testament,* but the end with the ink frozen in the inkwell gives a note on his life as a student which can never be ignored.

Villon had only one poetical theme—himself: his life and his sorrows about Paris, the university of which he was very proud, the intellectual life of his times, the life of the streets and of the court. In all of these he had a literary pride without reservations. The life of the court and the life of the streets and the cultured life of the student—as of the poet—were of the same block.

So that when the poet speaks of *The Fair Armoress* he was speaking of a woman he undoubtedly knew well, making his comments on the details of her life and of how the times have neglected her and himself.

But the pride of the sensitive man, shown in his poetic invention, forces itself directly on the eye in the course of his words. An artist, and the sensitivity of the artist can never have been more inviolately patent, more incontrovertible than in this student poet.

His mode is set. It was a subjective preoccupation; nothing else concerned him. In that narrow range he found his release. Typically French. Nothing could jar him from his track. That gave him all the freedom of invention he required.

But the pride of invention was his own, something that cannot be foretold. Nothing to do but follow the lead of the times which surrounded him, inventing with the sensitive ear with which he had been endowed and to which he clung—his comfort as an artist.

Direct is the word for every word that Villon set down. There was no intermediate field to his address. He was directly concerned in the affairs of his life, took his responsibilities deeply and, as he grew older, bitterly, but saw no reason to seek to avoid them or to confess them. He was a poet, needed no intermediary, secular or sacred. Indeed his first victim in a brawl was a priest. In his poems he speaks frequently of priests and of popes as of men he might well have met about the world, men on an equal footing with himself. He acknowledged no superior.

This direct approach to his material came, most likely, from the small world he inhabited, the Paris of his studenthood.

That directness of a wholly responsible man among his peers entered into the very structure of his verse. When he uses a figure of speech it was not "as if" but coming from *himself* in one of the "disguises" that the world forces us to wear: prince or pauper, rich man or groveler—except that no one could make him grovel even on the gibbet.

To Villon, any ruse, or indirect approach, even at the excuse of art, savored of the lie. Mallarmé's "beautiful" symbolistic inventions were the antithesis of Villon's nature. Say what you have to say until hell freezes over! When setting down his words, little mattered save for art, save for his art against which he measured the world's devices.

So that when a modern literary critic seeks an approach with which to compare current attitudes, he must think inevitably, most readily of Villon.

The immediacy and impatience with the disguises of history must appeal to a modern reader, making it particularly timely to have a new reading of his poems at the present—especially one that conveys their uncompromising nature and surpassing excellence as art. Nothing like them had ever been written in the past—in spite of his fifteenth-century critics and those who had followed them.

The name of Villon is peculiarly alive in our world today; there is immediacy about it that makes him a contemporary in all our lives. We can still learn from him how to write a poem.

A recent comment by a critic (Hugh Kenner) may be worth noting. *Le mot juste* had come up for discussion: it was justly stated that if there were the faintest feeling that Villon ever wrote to be effective, it would have destroyed the validity of what he had to say. *Le mot juste* is the *ready word*—it has no other significance. This is fundamental. In literature there can be no seeking for words. For a writer to so indulge himself is to tread dangerous ground. But good writing is rare. In Villon, if he had even been conscious of an alternative, if there ever were the faintest sense of his wanting to be effective, the game would have been up. It never occurred.

To him a man was a man. To have called him a "male" would have been completely misleading. The same in his use of the word "woman"... nothing to be confused about that. The term might be interpreted vulgarly, as perhaps in our own day; but Villon used it vulgarly when the necessity called for it.

He was the complete Frenchman in that, as well as the child of his times—the fifteenth century. Every nation of Europe, as well as of the Orient, had its own characteristic bias in its attitude toward woman; but Villon had the French, even the Parisian attitude, which marked him singularly.

The evasion of forthrightness was not found in Villon, it never occurred to him; but that he ignored sensitive sense perception was unthinkable. He was vigorous but not crude; his feelings for words, flooding over his writing (though he never evaluated it) is the quality of beauty, the beauty of his individual lines.

He was French, as French as was Rabelais. Briefly to the point—he was a Parisian much the same as we understand the term today. He was typically French—not French in association with Italian, which the English acquired through their Dante—but more of Chaucer of an earlier day when the English themselves were half French.

The French were, in their own minds, the most advanced people of their world, the most light-hearted, the gayest, most daring. They were Parisians—with Parisians' pride in their city, their city the center of the world and all the world of culture; and, no doubt, of fashion, and as well of the learning that went into its making.

It is important to emphasize that as a poet Villon was a student of the University not of Oxford, not Padua, but of Paris inhabited by the French! His pride in his city was something he could bite into. He was possessed by French devil-may-care, a French sensitivity—in such a song as the famous poem written on the gallows.

Freres humains qui après nous vivez

No one but a Frenchman (and a Parisian) could have written that song! Imagine anyone that would have had the qualities to bring off that song but Villon the Parisian, the young student.

And who but a Frenchman could have had the special feeling for the cocotte, for women, tender but daring; and as informed about them as shown in the ballade of *The Fair Armoress*. As well for *La Grosse Margot*: low down as it is, a typical French tart beautifully realized with all a Frenchman's artistry and wit and humor—and design.

A SHORT BIOGRAPHY

For centuries almost nothing was known about Villon except what scant facts could be gleaned from his poetry. Then in the 1870's scholars began leafing through contemporary documents and finding him mentioned, principally in the police records of the period. So in a sense it was thanks to his being a criminal that we know as much about him as we do.

He was born in Paris in 1431. His given name was François de Montcorbier (or François des Loges), and that of Villon he took from his protector. All we know about his father is that he was already dead when his son wrote the *Testament* in 1461. It seems likely that he died when Villon was an infant. His mother, though, was still alive when he wrote the *Testament*; he mentions her there with great tenderness, describes her as old, poor and illiterate, and makes her a present of one of his greatest ballades.

What his childhood was like, we can only imagine. He was born in the year that Joan of Arc was burned at the stake, when France, torn apart by the Hundred Years' War, was ruled by the still weak and ineffectual Charles VII. Not till Villon was five was Paris freed from English rule. This event brought some joy: there were magnificent processions through the streets, and in the next year, when the King made his entry into the city, there were great celebrations with mystery plays, and bonfires lit in the squares. But the country was in terrible shape. It was being ravaged by bands of unpaid men-at-arms, who ransacked anybody or anything they could lay their hands on.

Then too there was a series of calamities: in the year

before the English left there occurred one of the coldest winters the city had ever known (it snowed steadily for forty days); two years later there was a famine in which many died; then there was a windstorm which knocked down houses, chimneys and trees; then came a smallpox epidemic which was said to have killed some fifty thousand people, mostly children; then there were several years when wolves, goaded by hunger, entered Paris and killed children and even women. Villon could not have helped but have a close look at such things as death, starvation, cold and fear before he was seven.

At about that age, maybe a little earlier, he was sent to live with a certain Guillaume de Villon (the man whose name he took), a chaplain in the church of Saint-Benoît-le-Bétourné near the Sorbonne. This man fed him, clothed him, housed him, and gave him all his early education (such an arrangement was not uncommon in the Middle Ages). He must have treated the boy well; Villon mentions him with great fondness in the *Testament*, and speaks of some tight corners his protector helped him out of.

Sometime in his early teens he began studying at the University of Paris. In 1449 he got his Bachelor of Arts degree (roughly equivalent to our high school diploma), and in August of 1452 his Master of Arts (roughly equivalent to our B.A.). In spite of this array of degrees he was probably never a very good student. The University of Paris, too, had gone considerably downhill from its days of glory in the thirteenth century: it taught mainly a scholasticism so pedantic as to offer little attraction to a restless mind like Villon's, and the student body spent much of its time drinking, brawling and rioting—activities into which Villon undoubtedly entered with no lack of enthusiasm.

One of the famous student pranks of the fifteenth century occurred in the year before Villon graduated, and we are certain he took an active part in it.

In front of the house of a certain Mademoiselle de Bruyères there stood a stone, which had probably once been a boundary marker, called Le Pet-au-Deable (The Devil's Fart). Undoubtedly because of its name it was the subject of endless student jokes. Then one day they were seized with a desire to possess it, came in a great body and dragged it off to their domain on the Left Bank. Naturally Mademoiselle de Bruyères, being an officious, law-abiding citizen, trotted off to the police with her tale of woe. Shortly afterwards they went and got the stone, dragged it down to the Île-de-la-Cité, and placed it in the courtyard of the Palais Royal for safekeeping. But the students, who by now were just getting warmed up, broke into the courtyard one night, and dragged it back to the Left Bank. They then swiped another stone from in front of Mademoiselle de Bruyère's house, named it La Vesse (The Silent Fart), and also dragged it back to their domain, where they nightly performed mock ceremonial dances around it.

Then the students dreamed up another stunt. For years one of their favorite occupations had been swiping the house-signs which were so prevalent in Paris. Now they got the idea of performing mock marriages with these signs. They got *The Stag* to marry *The Bear* and *The Sow*. This was the last straw: the Provost, Robert d'Estouteville, got his men together, marched off to the street where the stones were, and piled them on a cart. His men broke into several houses containing insurgent students with their caches of stolen signs and assorted weapons. They took a lot of students prisoner, pushed people around considerably, pocketed various things that didn't belong to them, and drank whatever wine they found.

The University authorities were indignant, and the affair dragged on for years with all the bitterness of the many medieval clashes between the Church (here represented by the University) and the secular arm of the law.

Before leaving Villon's university days, one thing more must be mentioned. His having graduated gave him a curious half-clerical, half-lay status. He could wear his hair tonsured, and be tried (in theory at least) only by an ecclesiastical court. For a man who was perhaps contemplating a criminal career, this was of enormous importance; the ecclesiastical courts more often than not tried to protect their own rather than prosecute them.

And it was not long before he became involved in crime. In 1455, on the evening of Corpus Christi (June 5), he was sitting outside Saint-Benoît with some friends when along came a priest named Philippe Chermoye, who apparently was spoiling for a fight with Villon. Hot words immediately began to fly, and Chermoye struck him in the face with a large dagger, cutting his upper lip and causing a great flow of blood. Now Villon started to defend himself; he drew his own dagger, stabbed the priest in the groin, and then hurled a rock in his face. With Chermoye sprawled out on the ground, Villon left, first going to a barber to have his wound dressed and then leaving town on the correct assumption that the police would be after him. Chermoye was eventually taken to the Hôtel-Dieu where he died several days later.

What the fight was about has remained a mystery. There was a girl named Ysabeau sitting with Villon when it started. It might have been over her, but no one knows who she was.

In any case, friends petitioned for his pardon, working through two separate channels to make sure he got it. In January of 1456 both of them came through, one under the name of François de Montcorbier and the other under the name of François des Loges. Villon now could return to Paris.

Then towards Christmas of that same year two events of importance took place. First of all he wrote *The Legacy*. Up to then, as far as we know, he had only written several ballades and the lost *Romance of the Devil's Fart*, an account of the escapade with the stone marker. Now at twenty-five he produced his first major work. He did not yet have command of the range and power he was to display in his later works, but Villon's genius is already there, in flashes that are unmistakable.

The second event was the robbery of the College of Navarre. One night towards Christmas, five men met in the *Mule* tavern not far from Saint-Benoît. They were Villon, Guy Tabary, whom Villon claims was the copyist of the above-mentioned *Romance*, Dom Nicholas, a monk from Picardy, Colin de Cayeux, the son of a Parisian locksmith and, in the words of a subsequent deposition, *fortis operator crochetorum* (a powerful operator of picklocks), and Little John, *ejus socius, forcius operator* (his companion, who is even more skillful). After giving Tabary a lecture on keeping his mouth shut concerning what he was about to see, they paid up and left. They took a short stroll up the street, climbed one wall, left Tabary as lookout, climbed another wall, and then made their way across a courtyard into the College. They picked the locks of two coffers, one inside the other, and made off with the contents. Once outside again, they paid off Tabary and divided the rest among themselves.

Naturally there was an inquest, but the police made no headway, until the following spring Guy Tabary started on a talking spree that probably has rarely been equaled in the annals of crime. On several occasions he had drinks with a priest named Pierre Marchant from Paray and started boasting. The gist of his bragging was that he was "in with the boys" and had himself helped pull off some pretty big jobs, as for instance that one at the College of Navarre. He was even obliging enough to fill in a lot of details, and Marchant, as proud as punch of his new role of amateur detective, went trotting off to the Châtelet to tell the whole story. Naturally the police hauled Tabary in and started questioning him. At first he denied everything, but when they confronted him with Marchant's deposition he saw the jig was up. After a short but sufficient torture session he made a full confession. He was finally released and fined.

But now Villon, a wanted man in Paris, began four and a half years of self-imposed exile, wandering through much of France. We know very little about these years. Villon himself tells us that he first went to Angers (see *Legacy*, line 43 and note 3). At some point in his wandering he also took part as poet in the life of the court of Charles d'Orléans at Blois (see Misc. Poems VII and note). It is difficult to try to imagine the meeting of these two men, the finest poets of their time and yet so incredibly dissimilar: Charles d'Orléans, the disillusioned aging prince of royal blood who was a master of refined, subdued courtly poetry, and Villon, the young destitute criminal who wrote an intensely personal type of poetry, now lyric, now vitriolic, now sardonic. What their further relations were, and what was the occasion for Villon's writing the *Epistle* to this prince's daughter are still a mystery. (For a discussion of this see the note to Misc. Poems, VIII.)

Then all of a sudden in the summer of 1461 he turns up in Meung-sur-Loire in the prison of Thibault d'Auxigny, Bishop of Orléans. What crime it was that landed him there, we have no idea, but apparently the treatment he received was harsh enough to break his health. Somehow, while he was there he managed to write the *Epistle to his Friends* (Misc. Poems, IX). Then, by an extraordinary stroke of luck, on October 2 the new king, Louis XI, passed through Meung, and since it was the custom for prisoners to be released on a monarch's first entry into a city, Villon was set free.

After a trip to Moulins where he wrote the amusing *Request to the Duke of Bourbon* (Misc. Poems, X), he headed for the outskirts of Paris where he spent the winter of 1461-1462 hiding out and writing his masterpiece, *The Testament* (most of the ballades in it were probably written earlier), and soon afterwards the *Dialogue with his Heart* and *The Problem* (Misc. Poems, XI & XII).

Then he seems to have re-entered Paris, for in November 1462 we find him a prisoner in the Châtelet on a minor charge of theft. The offense was apparently not a serious one and he was about to be released, when the authorities of the University of Paris found out he was in jail and had him detained to settle the old account of the College of Navarre robbery. Fortunately for him, they were more interested in getting their money back than in prosecuting him. So they made him sign a bond that he would pay back 120 *écus* over a three-year period, and then released him.

But several weeks later he got into trouble again, this time seriously. One night he and three other fellows, after eating (and probably drinking a bit too much), walked up the Rue Saint-Jacques to go to Villon's room. On their way, one of these fellows, an ugly quarrelsome type, started an argument with a venerable papal scribe, Master François Ferrebouc, who was inside his scrivener's stall with his assistant scribes. A fight ensued in which Ferrebouc was wounded with a dagger. Villon, as soon as he had seen trouble brewing, had taken off, but unfortunately not soon enough, for Ferrebouc had recognized him.

Again he was thrown into the Châtelet, but this time it was no joke. His old friend and protector, Robert d'Estouteville, was no longer in charge, and the new Provost had no sympathy for the friends of the man he had replaced. The new Criminal Lieutenant, Pierre de la Dehors, was as tough as nails, and in addition Ferrebouc was not without influence. As a result Villon was tortured and finally sentenced to be "strangled and hanged on the gallows of Paris." Somehow during this period, probably the bleakest in his life, he found strength to compose his marvelous *Quatrain*, and one of his greatest lyrics, the *Epitaphe* (Misc. Poems, XIII & XIV).

His sentence, though, was flagrantly unjust. One man had only been wounded, and in a fight in which Villon had not taken part. He appealed to Parliament and won his case. On January 5, 1463, they handed down a decision annulling the Provost's sentence, but banishing Villon from Paris for ten years "in view of his bad character."

Free again, he wrote the *Panegyric to the Court of Parliament* asking for three days' grace to make preparations for leaving, and the wonderfully wise-cracking *Question to the Clerk of the Prison Gate* (Misc. Poems, XV & XVI). But what became of him then no one knows. He must have left Paris, but after that he disappears from history. Rabelais recounts two events that he claims happened to him in later life, but neither seems to have any more basis in fact than Rabelais' desire to spin a good yarn.

When he left Paris in that January of 1463, he was only thirty-two, but he probably appeared much older. Probably too, he was broken in health and spirit. He might have died on a mat of straw in some cheap tavern; or in a cold, dank cell; or in a fight in some dark street with another Coquillard; or perhaps, as he always feared, on a gallows in a little town in France. We will probably never know. But in the course of not much more than six years he had turned out a body of poetry great enough to leave him with few rivals in the literature of his own country or in that of any other.

A WORD ON THE
TEXT, TRANSLATION AND NOTES

The text printed here is based on that of the Longnon-Foulet edition (see the Bibliography on page 223), with some of the changes suggested by Burger in the introduction to his *Lexique* and only a few of Thuasne's emendations. I mention all this because the world is full of altered, modernized versions of Villon's poetry, which, as Wyndham Lewis says, are equivalent to The Girl's Shakespeare.

I have also used the titles Villon seems to have intended, as for instance *The Legacy* instead of *The Little Testament* and the *Testament* instead of *The Great Testament*. With the lyric pieces, though, some of the more familiar titles will be found in brackets alongside the original ones.

To anyone attempting to read the French text it is enormously important to have some idea of how to pronounce it. Without this, the reader can get little idea of Villon's sense of sound and poetic rhythm, which is extraordinary to say the least. The main rules to follow (that is, the principal differences between fifteenth-century and modern French) are:

1) r's were rolled as in Spanish or Italian.
2) -ill- was pronounced like the Spanish -ll- or the Italian -gli-, *not* -y- as today.
3) oi was pronounced wé, not wa as it is today. In other words his name was pronounced Franswé Villon, not Franswa Viyon as it is today.
4) All unaccented final e's were pronounced, even after another e. In other words, *matinée* had four syllables, not three as it would today.

This list, although by no means complete, covers what is important, and anyone who keeps these rules in mind will get a good idea of the sound of Villon's poetry.

The translation given here is as close to the original as readable free verse will allow. Prose was put aside as giving almost no feeling of the original, and rhymed metered verse was decided against firstly because the problems of French metrics and rhyme-schemes are so different from those of English as to make translation almost impossible; secondly because such an undertaking would be senseless in a bilingual edition.

The notes appended to the text are not there for "ritual adornment and terror" but to help the reader understand the poetry, many parts of which are incomprehensible or misleading without them. I have avoided scholarly discussions, and limited myself to what would inform or interest the reader.

Supernumerals in the French text refer to the notes at the back of the book. In the translation, an asterisk at the end of a stanza indicates that the original is annotated, and the reader has only to look across at the French to find the number of the note.

At the very end of the book there is a bibliography for anyone interested in doing further reading on Villon.

I have also included a fifteenth-century musical setting to one of Villon's rondeaux (see page 200). So far as I know, this is the first time that it has been printed with an edition of Villon's works.

Anthony Bonner
New York, 1959

Le Lais / The Legacy

LE LAIS

I

L'an quatre cens cinquante six,
Je, Françoys Villon, escollier,
Considerant, de sens rassis,
Le frain aux dens, franc au collier,
Qu'on doit ses œuvres conseillier,
Comme Vegece[1] le raconte,
Sage Rommain, grant conseillier,
Ou autrement on se mesconte ...

II

En ce temps que j'ay dit devant,
Sur le Noel, morte saison,
Que les loups se vivent de vent
Et qu'on se tient en sa maison,
Pour le frimas, pres du tison,
Me vint ung vouloir de brisier
La tres amoureuse prison
Qui souloit mon cuer debrisier.

III

Je le feis en telle façon,
Voyant celle devant mes yeulx
Consentant a ma desfaçon,
Sans ce que ja luy en fust mieulx;
Dont je me dueil et plains aux cieulx,
En requerant d'elle venjance
A tous les dieux venerieux,
Et du grief d'amours allejance.

IV

Et se j'ay prins en ma faveur
Ces doulx regars et beaux semblans
De tres decevante saveur
Me trespersans jusques aux flans,
Bien ilz ont vers moy les piez blans
Et me faillent au grant besoing.
Planter me fault autres complans
Et frapper en ung autre coing.[2]

2

THE LEGACY

In the year fourteen fifty-six,
I, François Villon, man of letters,
sound in mind and body,
determined, willing, and believing
that other men must judge one's works,
as Vegetius has declared,
that wise Roman and great counsellor,
or else one goes astray...*   8

At this time, as I have said,
near Christmas, the dead season
when wolves live off the wind,
and people, fearing frost,
stay home near burning logs,
a desire came to me
to flee those bonds of love
from which my heart was breaking.   16

And this I did,
seeing her before me
consenting to my destruction,
and yet no happier therewith.
To heaven I lament and grieve,
demanding vengeance from all
the gods of love, and relief
from Love's afflictions.   24

And even though I showed some favor
to those sweet looks and fair appearances
which proved so treacherous
and pierced me to the quick,
they've left me now
and failed me in my greatest need.
I'd better cultivate another field
and mint a different kind of coin.*   32

* See page xxvi.

3

v Le regart de celle m'a prins
Qui m'a esté felonne et dure:
Sans ce qu'en riens aye mesprins,
Veult et ordonne que j'endure
La mort, et que plus je ne dure;
Si n'y voy secours que fouïr.
Rompre veult la vive souldure,
Sans mes piteux regretz oïr!

vi Pour obvier a ces dangiers,
Mon mieulx est, ce croy, de partir.
Adieu! Je m'en vois a Angiers:[3]
Puis qu'el ne me veult impartir
Sa grace, ne me departir.
Par elle meurs, les membres sains;
Au fort, je suis amant martir
Du nombre des amoureux sains.

vii Combien que le depart me soit
Dur, si faut il que je l'eslongne:
Comme mon povre sens conçoit,
Autre que moy est en quelongne,
Dont oncques soret de Boulongne
Ne fut plus alteré d'umeur.[4]
C'est pour moy piteuse besongne:
Dieu en vueille oïr ma clameur!

viii Et puis que departir me fault,
Et du retour ne suis certain
(Je ne suis homme sans desfault
Ne qu'autre d'acier ne d'estain,
Vivre aux humains est incertain
Et après mort n'y a relaiz,
Je m'en vois en pays loingtain),
Si establis ce present laiz.

ix Premierement, ou nom du Pere,
Du Filz et du Saint Esperit,
Et de sa glorieuse Mere
Par qui grace riens ne perit,
Je laisse, de par Dieu, mon bruit
A maistre Guillaume Villon,[5]
Qui en l'onneur de son nom bruit,
Mes tentes et mon pavillon.[6]

4

Those looks of hers ensnared me,
she who's been false and cruel,
and though I've done no wrong,
she wishes and commands I suffer
death, and be no more—
there's little I can do but flee.
She wants to break the vital bond
without hearing my wretched moans.   40

To avoid such dangers, it would,
I think, be best to leave.
Good-by! I'm off to Angers,
since I can't have her favor,
nor even one small part of it.
Through her I die, and yet my body's
sound; I am a martyred lover
among the saints of Love.*   48

As hard as it may be for me
to go, I must now leave her.
As my feeble mind sees things,
someone else has caught her eye,
which makes my throat more parched
than that of any herring from Boulogne.
What a wretched business!
May God deign to hear my cry!*   56

And since I now must go
without assurance of returning,
(I'm not without my faults, nor made
of tougher stuff than other men;
human life is an uncertain thing
and there's no respite from death;
also, I have far to go),
I now set forth this will.   64

First, in the name of the Father,
the Son and the Holy Ghost,
and of His Glorious Mother
by whose grace none perish,
I leave, God willing, to Master
Guillaume Villon my reputation
(which in his name shines forth),
my tents and my pavilions.*   72

5

x Item, a celle que j'ai dit,
 Qui si durement m'a chassié
 Que je suis de joye interdit
 Et de tout plaisir dechassié,
 Je laisse mon cuer enchassié,
 Palle, piteux, mort et transy:
 Elle m'a ce mal pourchassié,
 Mais Dieu luy en face mercy!

xi Item, a maistre Ythier Marchant,[7]
 Auquel je me sens tres tenu,
 Laisse mon branc d'acier tranchant,
 Ou a maistre Jehan le Cornu,[8]
 Qui est en gaige detenu
 Pour ung escot huit solz montant;
 Si vueil, selon le contenu,
 Qu'on leur livre, en le rachetant.

xii Item, je laisse a Saint Amant[9]
 Le Cheval Blanc, avec *la Mulle*,
 Et a Blarru[10] mon dyamant
 Ou *l'Asne Royé* qui reculle.
 Et le decret qui articulle
 Omnis utriusque sexus,
 Contre la Carmeliste bulle
 Laisse aux curez, pour mettre sus.[11]

xiii Et a maistre Robert Valee,[12]
 Povre clerjot en Parlement,
 Qui n'entent ne mont ne vallee,
 J'ordonne principalement
 Qu'on luy baille legierement
 Mes brayes, estans aux *Trumillieres*,
 Pour coeffer plus honnestement
 S'amye Jehanne de Millieres.

xiv Pour ce qu'il est de lieu honneste,
 Fault qu'il soit mieulx recompensé,
 Car le Saint Esperit l'admoneste,
 Obstant ce qu'il est insensé;
 Pour ce, je me suis pourpensé,
 Puis qu'il n'a sens ne qu'une aulmoire,
 A recouvrer sur Maupensé,
 Qu'on lui baille l'Art de Memoire.

Item: to the lady I have mentioned,
who drove me out so cruelly
as to cut me off from joy
and banish me from pleasure,
I leave my heart enshrined,
pale, piteous, cold and dead.
She brought this fate upon me;
may God show her mercy.   80

Item: to Master Ythier Marchant,
to whom I feel obliged (or else
to Master Jean le Cornu,) I leave
my sword of razored steel, which is
in pawn right now for just eight *sous*.
I express my wish, hereby,
that it be given them—
once they've paid the price.*   88

Item: I bequeath to Saint-Amand
The White Horse and *The She-Mule*;
and to Blaru my diamond,
or the balking *Zebra*.
And the itemized decree,
Omnis utriusque sexus, against the bull
for Carmelites, I bequeath
to priests—let them enforce it.*   96

And to Master Robert Vallée,
poor young clerk in Parliament,
who can't tell hill from dale,
I first of all command
that he be given right away
my pants, which are in *The Greaves*,
so he can clothe more decently
his mistress, Jeanne de Milières.*   104

Since his family's well-to-do,
he must be better recompensed
(thus the Holy Ghost would have it,
seeing he is somewhat cracked).
I've thought it over and decided
that since a closet has more brains
than he, let Tom Fool
give him *The Art of Memory*.   112

7

xv   Item, pour assigner la vie
Du dessusdit maistre Robert,
(Pour Dieu, n'y ayez point d'envie!)
Mes parens, vendez mon haubert,
Et que l'argent, ou la plus part,
Soit emploié, dedans ces Pasques,
A acheter a ce poupart
Une fenestre emprès Saint Jaques.

xvi   Item, laisse et donne en pur don
Mes gans et ma hucque de soye
A mon amy Jacques Cardon,[13]
Le glan aussi d'une saulsoye,
Et tous les jours une grasse oye
Et ung chappon de haulte gresse,
Dix muys de vin blanc comme croye,
Et deux procès, que trop n'engresse.

xvii   Item, je laisse a noble homme,
Regnier de Montigny,[14] trois chiens;
Aussi a Jehan Raguier[15] la somme
De cent frans, prins sur tous mes biens.
Mais quoy? Je n'y comprens en riens
Ce que je pourray acquerir:
On ne doit trop prendre des siens,
Ne son amy trop surquerir.

xviii   Item, au seigneur de Grigny[16]
Laisse la garde de Nijon,
Et six chiens plus qu'a Montigny,
Vicestre, chastel et donjon;
Et a ce malostru chanjon,
Mouton,[17] qui le tient en procès,
Laisse trois coups d'ung escourjon,
Et couchier, paix et aise, es ceps.

xix   Et a maistre Jaques Raguier[18]
Laisse l'Abruvouër Popin,
Pesches, poires, seur gras figuier,
Tousjours le chois d'ung bon loppin,
Le trou de *la Pomme de Pin*,
Clos et couvert, au feu la plante,
Emmailloté en jacoppin;
Et qui voudra planter, si plante.

8

Item: to help said Master Robert
gain some sort of livelihood
(for God's sake don't be envious),
my parents are to sell my coat of mail,
and, before Easter, use the money,
or at least the better part of it,
to buy this simpleton a stall
near Saint-Jacques.   120

Item: I bequeath in outright gift
my gloves and silk cape
to Jacques Cardon, my friend,
and an acorn from a willow grove,
and every day a plump goose
and a capon rich in fat,
ten hogheads of wine as white as chalk,
and two lawsuits—so he won't get too fat.*   128

Item: I leave that nobleman,
Regnier de Montigny, three dogs;
and to Jean Raguier a hundred
francs deducted from my property,
but as it stands right now, not
including any later increase—a man
should not expect too much from friends,
or sponge too much from them.*   136

Item: to the lord of Grigny
I leave the guard of Nigeon,
and six dogs more than Montigny,
and castle and dungeon of Bicêtre;
and to that ill-starred bastard,
Mouton, who's fighting him in court,
I leave three lashes of a leather thong,
and peaceful sleep with feet in irons.*   144

And to Master Jacques Raguier
I bequeath the Popin trough,
pears and peaches from a fat fig-tree,
choice and juicy morsels always,
and the *Pine-Cone Tavern* where he'll
be snug, his feet beside the fire,
wrapped in his Jacobin mantle,
letting the world laugh as it may.*   152

9

XX   Item, a maistre Jehan Mautaint
Et maistre Pierre Basanier,[19]
Le gré du seigneur qui attaint
Troubles, forfaiz, sans espargnier;
Et a mon procureur Fournier,[20]
Bonnetz cours, chausses semelees,
Taillees sur mon cordouannier,
Pour porter durant ces gelees.

XXI   Item, a Jehan Trouvé,[21] bouchier,
Laisse *le Mouton* franc et tendre,
Et ung tacon pour esmouchier
Le Beuf Couronné qu'on veult vendre,
Et *la Vache*: qui pourra prendre
Le vilain qui la trousse au col,
S'il ne la rent, qu'on le puist pendre
Et estrangler d'ung bon licol!

XXII   Item, au Chevalier du Guet,
Le Hëaulme luy establis;
Et aux pietons qui vont d'aguet
Tastonnant par ces establis,
Je leur laisse deux beaux rubis
La Lanterne a la Pierre au Let.
Voire, mais j'auray *les Troys Lis*,
S'ilz me mainent en Chastellet.[22]

XXIII   Item, a Perrenet Marchant,[23]
Qu'on dit le Bastart de la Barre,
Pour ce qu'il est tres bon marchant,
Luy laisse trois gluyons de fuerre
Pour estendre dessus la terre
A faire l'amoureux mestier,
Ou il luy fauldra sa vie querre,
Car il ne scet autre mestier.

XXIV   Item, au Loup et a Cholet[24]
Je laisse a la fois ung canart
Prins sur les murs, comme on souloit,
Envers les fossez, sur le tart,
Et a chascun ung grant tabart
De cordelier jusques aux piez,
Busche, charbon et poix au lart,
Et mes houseaulx sans avantpiez.

Item: to Master Jean Mautaint
and Master Pierre Basanier
the goodwill of him who's so severe
in prosecuting crimes;
to my attorney, Fournier,
some caps and leather hose
fashioned at my cobbler's
to wear these icy days.*   160

Item: to the butcher Jean Trouvé
I leave *The Sheep*, fat and tender,
and a swatter, to keep the flies off
The Crowned Ox, which is for sale,
and *The Cow* too. Maybe he could catch
the guy who's carrying her away;
if that crook won't bring her back,
let's hope he's strangled in a harness.*   168

Item: to the Captain of the Watch
I assign *The Helmet*,
and to his men on foot,
groping past dark stalls,
I give two lovely rubies, and *The Lantern*
in the street named *Pierre-au-Lait*;
yes, but I'll have the *Three Lily* cell
if they take me to the Châtelet.*   176

Item: to Perrenet Marchant
who's called the Bâtard de la Barre,
because he's such a first-class merchant
I give him three bales of straw
to lay out on the ground
and carry out his lover's business;
otherwise he'll have to start in begging,
for he knows no other trade.*   184

Item: to The Wolf and to Cholet—
I leave them both a duck, taken from
the walls, the way we used to do it,
inside the moats, towards dark;
and to each a long Franciscan
cloak, reaching to his feet,
firewood, charcoal, peas with pork-fat,
and my boots without their tops.*   192

11

XXV   De rechief, je laisse, en pitié,
A trois petis enfans tous nus[25]
Nommez en ce present traictié,
Povres orphelins impourveus,
Tous deschaussiez, tous desvestus
Et desnuez comme le ver;
J'ordonne qu'ilz soient pourveus,
Au moins pour passer cest yver:

XXVI   Premierement, Colin Laurens,
Girart Gossouyn et Jehan Marceau,
Despourveus de biens, de parens,
Qui n'ont vaillant l'ance d'ung seau,
Chascun de mes biens ung fesseau,
Ou quatre blans, s'ilz l'ayment mieulx.
Ilz mengeront maint bon morceau,
Les enfans, quant je seray vieulx!

XXVII   Item, ma nominacion,
Que j'ay de l'Université,
Laisse par resignacion
Pour seclurre d'aversité
Povres clers de ceste cité
Soubz cest *intendit* contenus;
Charité m'y a incité,
Et Nature, les voiant nus:

XXVIII   C'est maistre Guillaume Cotin
Et maistre Thibault de Victry,[26]
Deux povres clers, parlans latin,
Paisibles enfans, sans estry,
Humbles, bien chantans au lectry;
Je leur laisse sans recevoir
Sur la maison Guillot Gueuldry,
En attendant de mieulx avoir.

XXIX   Item, et j'adjoings a la crosse
Celle de la rue Saint Anthoine,
Ou ung billart de quoy on crosse,
Et tous les jours plain pot de Saine;
Aux pijons qui sont en l'essoine,
Enserrez soubz trappe volliere,[27]
Mon mirouër bel et ydoine
Et la grace de la geolliere.

And also, out of pity, I give
to three small, shivering children
cited hereinafter,
poor orphans, destitute,
without clothes or shoes,
as naked, all of them, as worms—
I order they be provided for, at least
enough to make it through this winter: *   200

first of all, to Girart Gossouyn,
Colin Laurens and Jean Marceau,
who are without possessions, have no parents,
and don't even own the handle of a bucket,
I leave to each a portion of my estate,
or, if they prefer, four *blancs*.
Then they'll be eating well, those
children, by the time I'm old.   208

Item: my letter of nomination
from the University
I bequeath by resignation
to help in times of need
some poor Parisian clerks
hereinafter mentioned;
charity incites me, and nature
too, seeing them so naked.   216

They are Master Guillaume Cotin
and Master Thibaud de Vitry,
two poor Latin-speaking clerks,
peaceful children, unquarrelsome,
humble, good singers in the choir;
I leave them to receive the rent
on Guillot Gueldry's house
till something better comes along. *   224

Item: in addition to their crosier
I give the one that's in Rue Saint-Antoine,
or a billiard cue to play with, and every day
a pot of water from the Seine.
And to those poor pigeons so badly
off, locked up in some bird-cage,
I bequeath my clear, untarnished mirror
and the jailer's wife's good graces. *   232

13

XXX   Item, je laisse aux hospitaux
Mes chassiz tissus d'arigniee,[28]
Et aux gisans soubz les estaux,
Chascun sur l'œil une grongniee,
Trembler a chiere renfrongniee,
Megres, velus et morfondus,
Chausses courtes, robe rongniee,
Gelez, murdris et enfondus.

XXXI   Item, je laisse a mon barbier
Les rongneures de mes cheveulx,
Plainement et sans destourbier;
Au savetier mes souliers vieulx,
Et au freppier mes habitz tieulx
Que quant du tout je les delaisse,
Pour moins qu'ilz ne cousterent neufz
Charitablement je leur laisse.

XXXII   Item, je laisse aux Mendians,[29]
Aux Filles Dieu et aux Beguines,
Savoureux morceaulx et frians,
Flaons, chappons, grasses gelines,
Et puis preschier les Quinze Signes,
Et abatre pain a deux mains.
Carmes chevauchent noz voisines,
Mais cela, ce n'est que du mains.

XXXIII   Item, laisse *le Mortier d'Or*
A Jehan, l'espicier, de la Garde,[30]
Une potence de Saint Mor,
Pour faire ung broyer a moustarde.
A celluy qui fist l'avant garde
Pour faire sur moy griefz exploiz,
De par moy saint Anthoine l'arde!
Je ne luy feray autre laiz.[31]

XXXIV   Item, je laisse a Merebeuf
Et a Nicolas de Louvieux,[32]
A chascun l'escaille d'ung œuf,
Plaine de frans et d'escus vieulx.
Quant au concierge de Gouvieulx,
Pierre de Rousseville, ordonne,
Pour le donner entendre mieulx,
Escus telz que le Prince donne.

Item: I bequeath the hospitals
my windows hung with spiders' webs,
and to people lying under street-stalls
a black eye to each of them—
let them tremble with sullen face,
thin, unshaven, shivering,
with scanty breeches and tattered coat,
frozen, battered and sopping wet.*   240

Item: I bequeath my barber
the clippings from my hair
in full and outright gift;
to the cobbler my old shoes;
to the ragman my clothes, such
as they will be when I abandon them.
I give these things in charity
(that's less than what they cost me new).   248

Item: I bequeath the Mendicants,
the *Filles-Dieu* and Beguines
luscious, dainty morsels,
custard pies, plump hens and capons;
and then to preach the Fifteen Signs
and beg their bread with greedy hands.
The Carmelites make love to neighbors'
wives, but that's of no importance.*   256

Item: I leave *The Golden Mortar* to Jean
de la Garde, who keeps a spice-shop,
and also a Saint-Maur crutch to use
as a pestle for making mustard.
To that other guy who started things
and brought on me such unjust misery,
may Saint Anthony burn him up!
He'll get no other legacy from me.*   264

Item: I bequeath Merbeuf
and Nicolas de Louviers—
to each of them an egg-shell
full of old *écus* and francs;
and to the warden of Gouvieux,
Pierre de Rousseville, I leave
(and let this be a lesson to him)
écus of the Prince's kind.*   272

XXXV Finablement, en escripvant,
   Ce soir, seulet, estant en bonne,
   Dictant ces laiz et descripvant,
   J'oïs la cloche de Serbonne,[33]
   Qui tousjours a neuf heures sonne
   Le Salut que l'Ange predit;
   Si suspendis et mis en bonne
   Pour prier comme le cuer dit.

XXXVI Ce faisant, je m'entroublié,
   Non pas par force de vin boire,
   Mon esperit comme lié;
   Lors je sentis dame Memoire[34]
   Reprendre et mettre en son aumoire
   Ses especes collateralles,
   Oppinative faulce et voire,
   Et autres intellectualles,

XXXVII Et mesmement l'estimative,
   Par quoy prospective nous vient,
   Similative, formative,
   Desquelles souvent il advient
   Que, par leur trouble, homme devient
   Fol et lunatique par mois:
   Je l'ay leu, se bien m'en souvient,
   En Aristote aucunes fois.

XXXVIII Dont le sensitif s'esveilla
   Et esvertua Fantasie,
   Qui tous organes resveilla,
   Et tint la souvraine partie
   En suspens et comme amortie
   Par oppression d'oubliance
   Qui en moy s'estoit espartie
   Pour monstrer de Sens l'aliance.

XXXIX Puis que mon sens fut a repos
   Et l'entendement demeslé,
   Je cuidé finer mon propos;
   Mais mon ancre estoit gelé
   Et mon cierge trouvé soufflé;
   De feu je n'eusse peu finer;
   Si m'endormis, tout enmouflé,
   Et ne peus autrement finer.

Finally, tonight, while writing,
alone and in a pleasant mood,
composing and drawing up these legacies,
I heard the Sorbonne bell
which, at nine o'clock, always rings
the Salvation the Angel prophesied;
so I paused, and ceased my work
to pray as my heart wished.*   280

With this, I started dozing off
(not from any wine I'd drunk),
my mind as if transfixed;
then I saw Dame Memory
take up and place in shelves
her dependent species, and those
opinative, false and true,
and others intellectual.*   288

And also those estimative
wherewith we make provision,
and those conceptual or formative
by which it oft befalls
that when disturbed a man
turns mad and lunatic each month.
I read this, if my memory serves
me right, in Aristotle.   296

Then sensation roused itself
and next incited Fantasy,
which woke all other organs
and held that sovereign part
suspended, near to death
by oppression of forgetfulness
which was dispersed through me
to prove itself allied with Sense.   304

After my mind had come to rest
and my wits begun to clear,
I tried to end this work,
but my ink was frozen,
my candle-flame blown out.
Since I could get no other light,
I fell asleep with mittens on,
and thus I could not finish.   312

17

XL   Fait au temps de ladite date
Par le bien renommé Villon,
Qui ne menjue figue ne date.
Sec et noir comme escouvillon,
Il n'a tente ne pavillon
Qu'il n'ait laissié a ses amis,
Et n'a mais qu'ung peu de billon
Qui sera tantost a fin mis.

Done on the date above-mentioned
by the well-renowned Villon
who eats no figs or dates, and who's
dried-up and black as a baker's mop.
All his tents and his pavilions
he has left to friends; he now
has nothing but a little change,
and that too will soon be gone. 320

Le Testament / The Testament

LE TESTAMENT

I   En l'an de mon trentiesme aage,
Que toutes mes hontes j'eus beues,
Ne du tout fol, ne du tout sage,
Non obstant maintes peines eues,
Lesquelles j'ay toutes receues
Soubz la main Thibault d'Aussigny...[35]
S'evesque il est, seignant les rues,
Qu'il soit le mien je le regny.

II   Mon seigneur n'est ne mon evesque,
Soubz luy ne tiens, s'il n'est en friche;
Foy ne luy doy n'hommage avecque,
Je ne suis son serf[36] ne sa biche.
Peu m'a d'une petite miche
Et de froide eaue tout ung esté;
Large ou estroit, moult me fut chiche:
Tel luy soit Dieu qu'il m'a esté!

III   Et s'aucun me vouloit reprendre
Et dire que je le mauldis,
Non fais, se bien le scet comprendre;
En riens de luy je ne mesdis.
Vecy tout le mal que j'en dis:
S'il m'a esté misericors,
Jhesus, le roy de Paradis,
Tel luy soit a l'ame et au corps!

IV   Et s'esté m'a dur et cruel
Trop plus que cy ne le raconte,
Je vueil que le Dieu eternel
Luy soit donc semblable a ce compte...
Et l'Eglise nous dit et compte
Que prions pour noz ennemis!
Je vous diray: « J'ay tort et honte,
Quoi qu'il m'ait fait, a Dieu remis! »

22

THE TESTAMENT

In this my thirtieth year,
having drunk my fill of shame,
being neither wholly wise nor foolish,
in spite of the many miseries
I've had, all of which have come
from the hands of Thibaud d'Auxigny . . .
If he's a bishop, blessing streets,
thank God, at least, that he's not mine.   8

He's not my lord or bishop, I hold
no land from him unless it's fallow;
I owe him no faith, nor any hommage
—I'm not his serf or doe.
He fed me on dry bread
and water one whole summer;
generous or stingy—to me he was
a miser; may God so be with him. *   16

Should someone try to blame me
and say I bring a curse on him,
I don't—let's make that clear.
In no way do I slander him;
the only evil that I speak is this:
if he has shown me mercy,
may Jesus, King of Paradise,
do likewise to his soul and body.   24

And if he's been more harsh and cruel
than I now care to tell,
then may the Lord Eternal
do the same to him. . .
But the Church tells us that we
must pray for our enemies,
and so I say, "I am wrong and shamed:
whatever he has done, let God be judge."   32

V   Si prieray pour luy de bon cuer,
Pour l'ame du bon feu Cotart.[37]
Mais quoy? ce sera donc par cuer,
Car de lire je suis fetart.
Priere en feray de Picart;
S'il ne la scet, voise l'aprendre,
S'il m'en croit, ains qu'il soit plus tart,
A Douai ou a l'Isle en Flandre!

VI   Combien, se oÿr veult qu'on prie
Pour luy, foy que doy mon baptesme!
Obstant qu'a chascun ne le crye,
Il ne fauldra pas a son esme.
Ou Psaultier prens, quant suis a mesme,
Qui n'est de beuf ne cordouen,
Le verselet escript septiesme
Du pséaulme *Deus laudem.*[38]

VII   Si prie au benoist fils de Dieu,
Qu'a tous mes besoings je reclame,
Que ma povre priere ait lieu
Vers luy, de qui tiens corps et ame,
Qui m'a preservé de maint blasme
Et franchy de ville puissance.
Loué soit il, et Nostre Dame,
Et Loÿs, le bon roy de France![39]

VIII   Auquel doint Dieu l'eur de Jacob
Et de Salmon l'onneur et gloire,
(Quant de proesse, il en a trop,
De force aussi, par m'ame! voire),
En ce monde cy transsitoire,
Tant qu'il a de long ne de lé,
Affin que de luy soit memoire,
Vivre autant que Mathusalé!

IX   Et douze beaux enfans, tous masles,
Véoir de son chier sang royal,
Aussi preux que fut le grant Charles,
Conceus en ventre nupcial,
Bons comme fut sainct Marcial![40]
Ainsi en preigne au feu Dauphin!
Je ne luy souhaitte autre mal,
Et puis Paradis en la fin.

Ɏ Thus, willingly, I'll pray for him,
on the soul of good Cotart, now dead.
But how then? It could only be by rote,
for I am lazy when it comes to reading.
I'll offer him a Picard's prayer, and if
he doesn't know it, he must learn it,
if he trusts me, before it is too late,
at Lille or Douai in Flanders.*   40

Ӿ However, if he wants my prayer
for him, provided he not tell
a soul, I give my word
he won't be disappointed.
When I have a psalter near at hand,
one bound in neither cordovan nor leather,
I'll take the seventh verse
of the *Deus Laudem* psalm.*   48

Ӿ So I pray to the blessed Son of God,
whom I invoke in all my needs,
that my poor prayer find favor
with Him, to whom I owe my soul and body,
and who has kept me from such misery
and delivered me from vile authority.
Let us praise Him, and Our Lady,
and France's good King Louis.*   56

Ɏ May God grant him Jacob's fortune
and Solomon's honor and glory
(as for prowess, he has enough,
and strength too, upon my soul)
in this transitory world, throughout
its length and breadth; and so
that he may be remembered, may he
live as long as did Methuselah.   64

And may he have twelve male children
sprung from his own royal blood
and conceived in nuptial womb,
heirs to Charlemagne's high courage
and braver than Saint Martial.
Thus let it befall the late
Dauphin; I wish him well—
may his end be in Paradise.*   72

X   Pour ce que foible je me sens
Trop plus de biens que de santé,
Tant que je suis en mon plain sens,
Si peu que Dieu m'en a presté,
Car d'autre ne l'ay emprunté,
J'ay ce testament tres estable
Faict, de derniere voulenté,
Seul pour tout et irrevocable.

XI   Escript l'ay l'an soixante et ung,
Lors que le roy me delivra
De la dure prison de Mehun,
Et que vie me recouvra,
Dont suis, tant que mon cuer vivra,
Tenu vers luy m'humilier,
Ce que feray jusques il moura
Bienfait ne se doit oublier.

XII   Or est vray qu'après plainz et pleurs
Et angoisseux gemissemens,
Après tristesses et douleurs,
Labeurs et griefz cheminemens,
Travail mes lubres sentemens,
Esguisez comme une pelote,
M'ouvrit plus que tous les Commens
D'Averroÿs sur Aristote.

XIII   Combien, au plus fort de mes maulx,
En cheminant sans croix ne pille,[41]
Dieu, qui les pelerins d'Esmaus
Conforta, ce dit l'Evangille,
Me monstra une bonne ville
Et pourveue du don d'esperance;
Combien que pecheur soie vile,
Riens ne hayt que perseverance.

XIV   Je suis pecheur, je le sçay bien;
Pourtant ne veult pas Dieu ma mort,
Mais convertisse et vive en bien,
Et tout autre que pechié mort.
Combien qu'en pechié soye mort,
Dieu vit, et sa misericorde,
Se conscience me remort,
par sa grace pardon m'accorde.

26

Since I feel myself so feeble,
poorer in possessions than in health,
and while my wits are still about me
(what little God has granted me,
for I have borrowed them from no one),
I've made this last will
and testament, once
and for all, irrevocable.   80

Written in this year of sixty-one
when the good King delivered me
from the harsh prison of Meung
and gave me back my life, for which,
as long as my heart lives, I shall
remain his humble servant,
and this until I die:
Good deeds should be remembered.   88

True, that after tears and cries
and groans of anguish,
after miseries and pains,
troubles and sad wanderings,
suffering has taught me better
than the Commentaries Averroës wrote
on Aristotle that my ideas were shaky,
my mind as dull and rounded as a ball.   96

However, amid my worst misfortunes,
wandering without a penny to my name,
God who comforted the pilgrims
at Emmaus, as the Gospel says,
showed me a goodly town
filled with the gift of hope.
However vile a sinner I may be,
God hates only those who persevere.*   104

I am a sinner, I know it well,
yet God wills not my death, but that
I should reform and live in righteousness,
I and others touched by sin.
Even though in sin I die,
God lives on with his great pity,
so if I should repent, I will be granted
pardon through His mercy.   112

27

XV   Et, comme le noble Rommant
De la Rose[42] dit et confesse
En son premier commencement
Qu'on doit jeune cuer en jeunesse,
Quant on le voit viel en viellesse,
Excuser, helas! il dit voir;
Ceulx donc qui me font telle presse
En meurté ne me vouldroient veoir.

XVI   Se, pour ma mort, le bien publique
D'aucune chose vaulsist mieulx,
A mourir comme ung homme inique
Je me jujasse, ainsi m'aist Dieux!
Griefz ne faiz a jeunes n'a vieulx,
Soie sur piez ou soie en biere:
Les mons ne bougent de leurs lieux,
Pour ung povre, n'avant n'arriere.

XVII   Ou temps qu'Alixandre regna,
Ung homs nommé Diomedès
Devant luy on luy amena,
Engrillonné poulces et des
Comme ung larron, car il fut des
Escumeurs que voions courir;
Si fut mis devant ce cadès,
Pour estre jugié a mourir.

XVIII   L'empereur si l'araisonna:
« Pourquoi es tu larron en mer? »
L'autre responce luy donna:
« Pourquoy laron me faiz clamer?
Pour ce qu'on me voit escumer.
En une petiote fuste?
Se comme toy me peusse armer,
Comme toy empereur je feusse.

XIX   « Mais que veux-tu? De ma fortune,
Contre qui ne puis bonnement,
Qui si faulcement me fortune,
Me vient tout ce gouvernement.
Excusez moy aucunement
Et saichiez qu'en grant povreté,
Ce mot se dit communement,
Ne gist pas grande loyauté. »

And as the noble *Romance*
of the Rose admits and states
in the lines with which it opens,
one must forgive young heart
its youth, when one sees it old
with age; and alas, it's true.
Those who track me down don't wish
to see me live to ripe old age.°   120

If by my death the public
weal might find some benefit,
I would condemn myself to die
in my iniquity, so help me God!
I make no grievances to young or old
whether I be on my feet or in the grave;
for a man that's poor, mountains
will move neither back nor forth.   128

In the days of Alexander's reign,
a man called Diomedes
was brought before the monarch,
his thumbs and fingers in irons
like a thief, for having been
a pirate on high seas;
thus he came before this judge
to be condemned to die.   136

The Emperor said to him,
"Why are you a robber on the sea?"
The other answered him,
"Why am I being called a robber?
Because some men have seen me
sail a little pirate ship?
If I could arm myself like you,
like you I'd be an emperor.   144

"But what can one expect? My way
of life comes from my fortune
which has falsely cast my lot
and against which I am helpless.
Please, then, have compassion,
and know that in great poverty
(as the saying goes)
lies no great loyalty."   152

29

XX
Quant l'empereur ot remiré
De Diomedès tout le dit:
« Ta fortune je te mueray
Mauvaise en bonne », si luy dit.
Si fist il. Onc puis ne mesdit
A personne, mais fut vray homme;
Valere pour vray le baudit,
Qui fut nommé le Grant a Romme.

XXI
Se Dieu m'eust donné rencontrer
Ung autre piteux Alixandre
Qui m'eust fait en bon eur entrer,
Et lors qui m'eust veu condescendre
A mal, estre ars et mis en cendre
Jugié me feusse de ma voix.
Necessité fait gens mesprendre
Et faim saillir le loup du bois.

XXII
Je plains le temps de ma jeunesse,
(Ouquel j'ay plus qu'autre gallé
Jusques a l'entree de viellesse),
Qui son partement m'a celé.
Il ne s'en est a pié allé
N'a cheval: helas! comment don?
Soudainement s'en est vollé
Et ne m'a laissié quelque don.

XXIII
Allé s'en est, et je demeure,
Povre de sens et de savoir,
Triste, failly, plus noir que meure,
Qui n'ay ne cens, rente, n'avoir;
Des miens le mendre, je dis voir,
De me desavouer s'avance,
Oubliant naturel devoir
Par faulte d'ung peu de chevance.

XXIV
Si ne crains avoir despendu
Par friander ne par leschier;
Par trop amer n'ay riens vendu
Qu'amis me puissent reprouchier,
Au moins qui leur couste moult chier.
Je le dy et ne croy mesdire;
De ce je me puis revenchier:
Qui n'a mesfait ne le doit dire.[43]

When the Emperor had thought
about Diomedes' words,
he said, "I shall change your fate
from bad to good"; and thus he did.
Nevermore Diomedes cursed anyone,
but instead became a worthy man.
Valerian, whom Romans called "The Great,"
vouches for this story's truth.   160

If God had granted me to meet another
Alexander as compassionate as this
to change my fortune for the better,
and after that had someone seen me sink
to evil, I would have then condemned myself
to have my body burned and turned to ashes.
Necessity causes men to err, and hunger
goads wolves snarling from the woods.   168

I regret those days of youth
(when, more than most, I had a life
of joy until old age came on)
which left me when my back was turned.
They didn't leave on foot, alas,
or horseback. But how then?
Suddenly they stole away,
and left me not a thing.   176

They've gone, and I remain,
poor in wits and knowledge,
sad, discouraged, more black than ripe,
without rent, income or possessions.
My most distant kin (I tell
the truth) now wishes to disown me,
forgetting natural duty, because
of some slight lack of fortune.   184

I've not squandered money eating
or indulging other pleasures of the flesh;
nor through too much loving have I sold
a thing for which my friends can blame me,
or at least nothing costing them too much.
I can say this with clear conscience;
of such at least I'm innocent; a man
who's done no wrong need not confess.*   192

XXV   Bien est verté que j'ay amé
Et ameroie voulentiers;
Mais triste cuer, ventre affamé
Qui n'est rassasié au tiers
M'oste des amoureux sentiers.
Au fort, quelqu'ung s'en recompence,
Qui est ramply sur les chantiers!
Car la dance vient de la pance.

XXVI   Hé! Dieu, se j'eusse estudié
Ou temps de ma jeunesse folle
Et a bonnes meurs dedié,
J'eusse maison et couche molle.
Mais quoi? je fuyoie l'escolle,
Comme fait le mauvais enfant.
En escripvant ceste parolle,
A peu que le cuer ne me fent.

XXVII   Le dit du Saige trop luy feiz
Favorable (bien en puis mais!)
Qui dit: « Esjoÿs toy, mon filz,
En ton adolescence »; mais
Ailleurs sert bien d'ung autre mes,
Car « Jeunesse et adolescence »,
C'est son parler, ne moins ne mais,
« Ne sont qu'abus et ignorance ».[44]

XXVIII   Mes jours s'en sont allez errant
Comme, dit Job, d'une touaille
Font les filetz, quant tisserant
En son poing tient ardente paille:
Lors, s'il y a nul bout qui saille,
Soudainement il le ravit.
Si ne crains plus que rien m'assaille,
Car a la mort tout s'assouvit.

XXIX   Ou sont les gracieux gallans
Que je suivoye ou temps jadis,
Si bien chantans, si bien parlans,
Si plaisans en faiz et en dis?
Les aucuns sont morts et roidis,
D'eulx n'est il plus riens maintenant:
Repos aient en paradis,
Et Dieu saulve le remenant!

It's true that I have loved,
and gladly would again;
but sad heart, and famished belly
not even partly satisfied
force me away from paths of love.
And so, let someone else take over
who has tucked away more food—
dancing is for men of nobler girth.   200

Good God, if I had studied
in the days of my mad youth
and been devoted more to virtue,
I now would have a house with downy bed.
But look! I ran away from school
just like a naughty child.
And now, as I write these words,
my heart is close to breaking.   208

I took the Sage's words too much
to heart (a lot of good it did me!),
those words which say, "Rejoice, my son,
while you are young," but in another
place he serves a different dish,
for "Youth and adolescence,"
he says—no more, no less—
"are naught but ignorance and vice."*   216

My days are quickly spent,
says Job, like threads from a piece
of cloth when the weaver
cuts them with a burning straw;
then, if some end still protrudes,
suddenly it's charred and gone.
Thus, I fear my fate no more,
for all things end with death.   224

Where are those laughing comrades
that I was with in former days,
who sang so well, talked so well
and so excelled in word and deed?
Some are dead and stiff—
nothing now remains of them;
may they find peace in Paradise,
and may God save the rest.   232

XXX   Et les autres sont devenus,
Dieu mercy! grans seigneurs et maistres;
Les autres mendient tous nus
Et pain ne voient qu'aux fenestres;
Les autres sont entrez en cloistres
De Celestins et de Chartreux,[45]
Botez, housez, com pescheurs d'oistres.
Voyez l'estat divers d'entre eux.

XXXI   Aux grans maistres Dieu doint bien faire,
Vivans en paix et en requoy;
En eulx il n'y a que refaire,
Si s'en fait bon taire tout quoy.
Mais aux povres qui n'ont de quoy,
Comme moy, Dieu doint patience!
Aux autres ne fault qui ne quoy,
Car assez ont pain et pitance.

XXXII   Bons vins ont, souvent embrochiez,
Saulces, brouetz et gros poissons,
Tartes, flans, oefz fritz et pochiez,
Perdus et en toutes façons.
Pas ne ressemblent les maçons,
Que servir fault a si grant peine:
Ilz ne veulent nuls eschançons,
De soy verser chascun se peine.

XXXIII   En cest incident me suis mis
Qui de riens ne sert a mon fait;
Je ne suis juge, ne commis
Pour pugnir n'absoudre mesfait:
De tous suis le plus imparfait,
Loué soit le doulx Jhesu Crist!
Que par moy leur soit satisfait!
Ce que j'ay escript est escript.

XXXIV   Laissons le moustier ou il est;[46]
Parlons de chose plus plaisante:
Ceste matiere a tous ne plaist,
Ennuyeuse est et desplaisante.
Povreté, chagrine, dolente,
Tousjours, despiteuse et rebelle,
Dit quelque parolle cuisante;
S'elle n'ose, si le pense elle.

,And the others have become,
thank God, great lords and masters;
yet other beg naked, and the only
bread they see is out of reach in shops;
yet others are in cloisters
among Carthusians or Celestines,
with boots like oyster-fishermen.
Look what different fates men have!*   240

May God grant great men good works,
and a life of peace and quiet.
There's no correcting men like them
so it's better not to say a word.
But to the poor who, like me,
have nothing, God grant them patience!
The others do not lack a thing—
they have their bread and rations.   248

They have good wines, straight from casks,
sauces, broths and fat fish,
tarts, custards, eggs poached, fried,
scrambled, and cooked all sorts of ways.
They're not like masons
who must be served so much;
they'd rather not trust waiters,
but let each man pour his own.   256

I've got involved in this digression
which is rather off the track;
I'm not a judge, nor the one
to punish or absolve misdeeds.
Of all, I am the most imperfect,
may sweet Jesus Christ be praised!
May they through me achieve atonement!
What I have written, I have written.   264

Let's leave churches where they are
and talk about more pleasant things;
not everyone enjoys this topic—
some find it boring and unpleasant.
Sad, wretched poverty, scornful
and rebellious, always has
biting words to say, which if she
doesn't dare to speak, she thinks.*   272

XXXV   Povre je suis de ma jeunesse,
De povre et de petite extrace;
Mon pere n'eust oncq grant richesse,
Ne son ayeul, nommé Orace;
Povreté tous nous suit et trace.
Sur les tombeaulx de mes ancestres,
Les ames desquelz Dieu embrasse!
On n'y voit couronnes ne ceptres.

XXXVI   De povreté me garmentant,
Souventesfois me dit le cuer:
« Homme, ne te doulouse tant
Et ne demaine tel douleur,
Se tu n'as tant qu'eust Jaques Cuer:[47]
Mieulx vault vivre soubz gros bureau
Pouvre, qu'avoir esté seigneur
Et pourrir soubz riche tombeau! »

XXXVII   Qu'avoir esté seigneur!... Que dis?
Seigneur, lasse! ne l'est il mais?
Selon les davitiques dis
Son lieu ne congnoistra jamais.[48]
Quant du surplus, je m'en desmetz:
Il n'appartient a moy, pecheur;
Aux theologiens le remetz,
Car c'est office de prescheur.

XXXVIII   Si ne suis, bien le considere,
Filz d'ange portant dyademe
D'estoille ne d'autre sidere.
Mon pere est mort, Dieu en ait l'ame!
Quant est du corps, il gist soubz lame.
J'entens que ma mere mourra,
El le scet bien, la povre femme,
Et le filz pas ne demourra.

XXXIX   Je congnois que povres et riches,
Sages et folz, prestres et laiz,
Nobles, villains, larges et chiches,
Petiz et grans, et beaulx et laiz,
Dames a rebrassez colletz,
De quelconque condicion,
Portans atours et bourreletz,[49]
Mort saisit sans excepcion.

36

Poor I am from childhood,
from a poor and humble family;
my father never had great wealth,
nor did his grandfather, named Horace;
poverty tracks and follows us.
On the tombs of all my ancestors
(may God receive their souls!)
one sees no crowns or sceptres.   280

Often, as I bemoan
this poverty, my heart tells me,
"O mortal man, do not grieve
so much, nor show such sorrow
that you have less than did Jacques Coeur.
Better to dress in poor, coarse cloth
than once to have been a mighty lord
and now rot beneath a splendid tomb."*   288

To have been a lord! . . . What did I say?
A lord, alas! Is he no longer one?
According to the Psalms of David,
his place shall know of him no more.
As for the rest, I leave it;
it's not for sinners such as me;
to the theologians I refer the matter,
for it's a preacher's task.*   296

No I'm not, I'm well aware,
an angel's son with diadem
of stars or constellations.
My father's dead, God rest his soul,
his body lying under gravestone.
They say my mother too will die
(the poor old woman knows it well),
and the son will not be long.   304

I know that rich and poor,
fools and wisemen, priests and laymen,
nobles, peasants, princes and misers,
small and large, fair and ugly,
ladies with upturned collars,
and of any class whatever, wearing
costly hats or simple bonnets,
Death seizes without exception.*   312

37

XL

Et meure Paris ou Helaine,
Quiconques meurt, meurt a douleur
Telle qu'il pert vent et alaine;
Son fiel se creve sur son cuer,
Puis sue, Dieu scet quelle sueur!
Et n'est qui de ses maux l'alege:
Car enfant n'a, frere ne seur,
Qui lors voulsist estre son plege.

XLI

La mort le fait fremir, pallir,
Le nez courber, les vaines tendre,
Le col enfler, la chair mollir,
Joinctes et nerfs croistre et estendre.
Corps femenin, qui tant es tendre,
Poly, souef, si precieux,
Te fauldra il ces maux attendre?
Oy, ou tout vif aller es cieulx.

BALLADE[50]
(des dames du temps jadis)

Dictes moy ou, n'en quel pays,
Est Flora la belle Rommaine,
Archipiades, ne Thaïs,
Qui fut sa cousine germaine,
Echo parlant quant bruyt on maine
Dessus riviere ou sus estan,
Qui beaulté ot trop plus qu'humaine.
Mais ou sont les neiges d'antan?

Ou est la tres sage Helloïs,
Pour qui chastré fut et puis moyne
Pierre Esbaillart a Saint Denis?
Pour son amour ot ceste essoyne.
Semblablement, ou est la royne
Qui commanda que Buridan
Fust geté en ung sac en Saine?
Mais ou sont les neiges d'antan?

χᵐ Paris dies, and Helen too;
whoever dies, dies in pain
such that breath fails him:
his spleen bursts upon his heart,
he sweats—good God, what sweat!—
and no one can relieve him in his agony;
for he has no brother, child or sister
who in that moment wants to take his place.   320

χᵐ Death makes him tremble and turn white,
curls his nostrils, stretches taut his veins,
puffs out his neck, makes flesh turn flabby,
joints and nerves dilate and swell.
O woman's body, so tender,
smooth, soft and precious,
do these ills await you too?
Yes, unless you go alive to heaven.   328

BALLADE*
(of the Ladies of Bygone Times)

Tell me where, or in what land
is Flora the lovely Roman,
or Archipiada, or Thaïs
who so resembled her,
or Echo speaking when one called
across still pools or rivers,
and whose beauty was more than human.
But where are the snows of bygone years?   336

Where is Héloïse, so wise, for whom
Pierre Abelard was gelded
and made a monk at Saint-Denis?
For her love he bore these trials.
And where now is that queen
by whose command Buridan
was thrown in a sack in the Seine?
But where are the snows of bygone years?   344

La royne Blanche comme lis
Qui chantoit a voix de seraine,
Berte au grant pié, Bietris, Alis,
Haremburgis qui tint le Maine,
Et Jehanne la bonne Lorraine
Qu'Englois brulerent a Rouan;
Ou sont ilz, ou, Vierge souvraine?
Mais ou sont les neiges d'antan?

Prince, n'enquerez de sepmaine
Ou elles sont, ne de cest an,
Qu'a ce reffrain ne vous remaine:
Mais ou sont les neiges d'antan?

AUTRE BALLADE[51]
(*des seigneurs du temps jadis*)

Qui plus, ou est le tiers Calixte,
Dernier decedé de ce nom,
Qui quatre ans tint le papaliste?
Alphonce le roy d'Arragon,
Le gracieux duc de Bourbon,
Et Artus le duc de Bretaigne,
Et Charles septiesme le bon?
Mais ou est le preux Charlemaigne?

Semblablement, le roy Scotiste
Qui demy face ot, ce dit on,
Vermeille comme une amatiste
Depuis le front jusqu'au menton?
Le roy de Chippre de renon,
Helas! et le bon roy d'Espaigne
Duquel je ne sçay pas le nom?
Mais ou est le preux Charlemaigne?

D'en plus parler je me desiste;
Le monde n'est qu'abusion.
Il n'est qui contre mort resiste
Ne qui treuve provision.
Encor fais une question:
Lancelot le roy de Behaigne,
Ou est il? Ou est son tayon?
Mais ou est le preux Charlemaigne?

Queen Blanche as white as a lily
and who sang with mermaid's voice,
Big-footed Bertha, Beatrice, Alice,
Arembourg who held Maine,
and good Joan of Lorraine
whom the English burnt at Rouen;
where are they, where, O Sovereign Virgin?
But where are the snows of bygone years?   352

Prince, do not ask in a week
or yet in a year where they are;
I could only give this refrain:
but where are the snows of bygone years?   356

ANOTHER BALLADE*
(of the Lords of Bygone Times)

And now where is the third Callixtus,
last deceased of that name,
who four years held the papal throne?
Alfonso the King of Aragon,
the gracious Duke of Bourbon,
and Arthur, Britanny's duke,
and good Charles the Seventh of France?
But where is the bold Charlemagne?   364

Likewise, where is that Scottish king,
half of whose face, they say,
was as red as an amethyst
from his forehead down to his chin?
And Cyprus' famous king,
alas! and the good king of Spain
whose name I do not know?
But where is the bold Charlemagne?   372

But I must stop talking of this;
the world is only illusion.
No one stands up against death,
nor staves off its approach.
But just one more question:
Ladislaus, King of Bohemia,
where is he? Where is his grandfather?
But where is the bold Charlemagne?   380

Ou est Claquin le bon Breton?
Ou le conte Daulphin d'Auvergne
Et le bon feu duc d'Alençon?
Mais ou est le preux Charlemaigne?

AUTRE BALLADE[52]
(en vieil langage françoys)

Car, ou soit ly sains apostolles,
D'aubes vestus, d'amys coeffez,
Qui ne saint fors saintes estolles
Dont par le col prent ly mauffez
De mal talant tout eschauffez,
Aussi bien meurt que cilz servans,
De ceste vie cy bouffez:
Autant en emporte ly vens.

Voire, ou soit de Constantinobles
L'emperieres au poing dorez,
Ou de France ly roy tres nobles
Sur tous autres roys decorez,
Qui pour ly grans Dieux aourez
Bastist eglises et couvens,
S'en son temps il fut honnorez,
Autant en emporte ly vens.

Ou soit de Vienne et de Grenobles
Ly Dauphin, ly preux, ly senez,
Ou de Dijon, Salins et Doles,
Ly sires et ly filz ainsnez,
Ou autant de leurs gens privez,
Heraulx, trompetes, poursuivans,
Ont ilz bien bouté soubz le nez?
Autant en emporte ly vens.

Princes a mort sont destinez,
Et tous autres qui sont vivans;
S'ilz en sont courciez n'ataynez,
Autant en emporte ly vens.

Where is Guesclin, the good Breton knight,
or Dauphin, Count of Auvergne,
and the late brave Duke d'Alençon?
But where is the bold Charlemagne?   384

ANOTHER BALLADE*
(in Old French)

Now where is the saintly Pope
wearing his alb and amice, who only
girds himself with saintly stole,
and who, beside himself with rage,
takes the Devil by the neck?
He too must die, like any servant,
and have his life snuffed out:
even so must the wind take all.   392

Yes, and where is Constantinople's
Emperor with the golden fist,
or the most noble King of France,
glorious above all other kings,
who, for love of God, has
churches built, and convents.
If in his day men honored him,
even so must the wind take all.   400

Where is the Dauphin of Grenoble
or of Vienne, so wise and valiant,
or the lords of Dijon, Salins
or of Doles and their eldest sons,
or as many of their attendants,
heralds, pages, trumpeters? Have they
had their fill of wine and food?
Even so must the wind take all.   408

Princes have a destiny of death,
and all others now alive;
should this annoy or anger them,
even so must the wind take all.   412

XLII   Puis que papes, roys, filz de roys
Et conceus en ventres de roynes,
Sont ensevelis mors et frois,
En autruy mains passent leurs regnes,
Moy, povre mercerot de Renes,
Mourray je pas? Oy, se Dieu plaist;
Mais que j'aye fait mes estrenes,
Honneste mort ne me desplaist.

XLIII   Ce monde n'est perpetuel,
Quoy que pense riche pillart:
Tous sommes soubz mortel coutel.
Ce confort prent povre viellárt,
Lequel d'estre plaisant raillart
Ot le bruit, lors que jeune estoit,
Qu'on tendroit a fol et paillart,
Se, viel, a railler se mettoit.

XLIV   Or luy convient il mendier,
Car a ce force le contraint.
Regrete huy sa mort et hier,
Tristesse son cuer si estraint;
Se, souvent, n'estoit Dieu qu'il craint,
Il feroit ung orrible fait;
Et advient qu'en ce Dieu enfraint
Et que luy mesmes se desfait.

XLV   Car s'en jeunesse il fut plaisant,
Ores plus riens ne dit qui plaise:
Tousjours viel cinge est desplaisant,
Moue ne fait qui ne desplaise;
S'il se taist, affin qu'il complaise,
Il est tenu pour fol recreu;
S'il parle, on luy dit qu'il se taise
Et qu'en son prunier n'a pas creu.

XLVI   Aussi ces povres fameletes
Qui vielles sont et n'ont de quoy,
Quant ilz voient ces pucelletes
Emprunter elles, a requoy
Ilz demandent a Dieu pourquoy
Si tost naquirent, n'a quel droit.
Nostre Seigneur se taist tout quoy,
Car au tancer il le perdroit.

Since popes, kings and sons of kings
conceived in wombs of queens
are buried dead and cold,
their reigns passed on to others,
I, poor peddler from Rennes,
will I not die? Yes, if it please God;
but as long as I have had my fun,
I have no fear of honest death.   420

This world is not perpetual, whatever
wealthy pilferers might think:
all of us are under mortal knife.
This may comfort that old man
who, when he was young, was known
as quite a wit; but now, in his
old age, if he began to jest
men would think him mad, depraved.   428

So now he must go out and beg;
his needs force him to do this.
But all the time he's sick
at heart and only wants to die;
were it not for fear of God
he might commit some awful deed.
Often these old men transgress
God's law and kill themselves.   436

For if when young he was amusing,
now nothing that he says is pleasant:
old monkeys always are offensive,
and their grimaces displeasing.
If, to please, he doesn't say
a word, people think he's senile;
if he speaks, he's told to shut
his mouth and stop his driveling.   444

And those poor women, too,
who are so old and penniless,
when they see young virgins
slyly take their place,
they ask God what right he had
to make them born so soon.
Our Lord is silent—he knows
with them He'd lose a war of words.   452

45

LA VIEILLE EN REGRETTANT
LE TEMPS DE SA JEUNESSE
(*Les regrets de la belle Hëaulmiere*)

XLVII   Advis m'est que j'oy regreter
La belle qui fut hëaulmiere,[53]
Soy jeune fille soushaitter
Et parler en telle maniere:
« Ha! vieillesse felonne et fiere,
Pourquoi m'as si tost abatue?
Qui me tient, qui, que ne me fiere,
Et qu'a ce coup je ne me tue?

XLVIII   « Tollu m'as la haulte franchise
Que beaulté m'avoit ordonné
Sur clers, marchans et gens d'Eglise:
Car lors il n'estoit homme né
Qui tout le sien ne m'eust donné,
Quoy qu'il en fust des repentailles,
Mais que luy eusse habandonné
Ce que reffusent truandailles.

XLIX   « A maint homme l'ay reffusé,
Qui n'estoit a moy grant sagesse,
Pour l'amour d'ung garson rusé,
Auquel j'en feiz grande largesse.
A qui que je feisse finesse,
Par m'ame, je l'amoye bien!
Or ne me faisoit que rudesse,
Et ne m'amoit que pour le mien.

L   « Si ne me sceut tant detrayner,
Fouler aux piez, que ne l'aymasse,
Et m'eust il fait les rains trayner,
S'il m'eust dit que je le baisasse,
Que tous mes maulx je n'oubliasse.
Le glouton, de mal entechié,
M'embrassoit... J'en suis bien plus grasse!
Que m'en reste il? Honte et pechié.

THE OLD WOMAN'S LONGING
FOR THE DAYS OF HER YOUTH
(*The Lament of the Belle Hëaulmiere*)

It seemed I heard the one
they called the Belle Hëaulmiere
complain, longing for the days
when she was young, and saying:
"Ah! You treacherous, fierce Old Age,
why have I been beaten down so soon?
Who will care if I strike myself
and with that blow give up my life?*   460

"You took away the great power
my beauty used to give me
over merchants, clerks and churchmen:
for then was no man born
who wouldn't give me all
he had (perhaps with some regrets),
knowing I would offer him
that which beggars now refuse.   468

"I turned down many men
(which wasn't very bright of me)
because I loved a wily boy
to whom I gave myself.
I occasionally deceived him, but on
my soul I swear I loved him!
He in turn was cruel to me
and only wanted what I earned.   476

"He could have dragged me through the mud
or trod me under foot—I would have loved him;
even had he crippled me, he only
had to order me to kiss him
for all my woes to be forgotten.
The glutton, his soul tainted with evil,
would embrace me. . . A lot of good it's done me!
What have I been left with? Sin and shame.   484

LI   « Or est il mort, passé trente ans,
Et je remains vielle, chenue.
Quant je pense, lasse! au bon temps,
Quelle fus, quelle devenue!
Quant me regarde toute nue,
Et je me voy si tres changiee,
Povre, seiche, megre, menue,
Je suis presque toute enragiee.

LII   « Qu'est devenu ce front poly,
Cheveulx blons, ces sourcils voultiz
Grant entroeil, ce regart joly,
Dont prenoie les plus soubtilz;
Ce beau nez droit grant ne petiz,
Ces petites joinctes oreilles,
Menton fourchu, cler vis traictiz,
Et ces belles levres vermeilles?

LIII   « Ces gentes espaulles menues,
Ces bras longs et ces mains traictisses,
Petiz tetins, hanches charnues,
Eslevees, propres, faictisses
A tenir amoureuses lisses;
Ces larges rains, ce sadinet
Assis sur grosses fermes cuisses,
Dedens son petit jardinet?

LIV   « Le front ridé, les cheveux gris,
Les sourcilz cheus, les yeulx estains,
Qui faisoient regars et ris
Dont mains meschans furent attains;
Nez courbes de beaulté loingtains,
Oreilles pendantes, moussues,
Le vis pally, mort et destains,
Menton froncé, levres peaussues:

LV   « C'est d'umaine beaulté l'issue!·
Les bras cours et les mains contraites,
Les espaulles toutes bossues;
Mamelles, quoy? toutes retraites;
Telles les hanches que les tetes;
Du sadinet, fy! Quant des cuisses
Cuisses ne sont plus, mais cuissetes
Grivelees comme saulcisses.

"And now he's dead these thirty years,
and I live on, gray-haired and old.
Oh, when I think of those good days,
what I was then—what I've since become!
When I look at my naked body
and see myself so changed,
poor, skinny, dried out and shrivelled,
I almost lose my mind.   492

"Where's the smooth forehead,
the blond hair, the arched eyebrows,
the doe-like eyes whose glance
could trap the cleverest men;
that fine nose, neither big nor small,
those little well-shaped ears,
the dimpled chin, the clear, pretty face,
and those beautiful crimson lips?   500

"Those lovely little shoulders,
the long arms and pretty hands,
the small breasts, the full hips,
high, smooth, and so well made
to enter tournaments of love;
those broad loins, the vulva set
in plump, firm thighs
within its little garden?   508

"Now my forehead's wrinkled, my hair gray,
my eyebrows drooping, my eyes clouded—
those eyes whose glance and laughter
was to many their undoing;
my nose is hooked—its beauty gone,
my ears hang down like moss,
my face is pale, dead, and faded,
my chin puckered, my lips withered.   516

"So this is human beauty's end!
The arms short, the fingers stiff,
the shoulders completely humped.
The breasts, you ask? All shrivelled—
hips and paps alike.
The vulva?—Horrors! The thighs
no longer thighs but skin and bone
mottled like some sausage.   524

49

LVI   « Ainsi le bon temps regretons
Entre nous, povres víelles sotes
Assises bas, a crouppetons,
Tout en ung tas comme pelotes,
A petit feu de chenevotes
Tost allumees, tost estaintes;
Et jadis fusmes si mignotes!
Ainsi en prent a mains et maintes. »

BALLADE[54]
(*La belle Hëaulmiere aux filles de joie*)

« Or y pensez, belle Gantiere
Qui m'escoliere souliez estre,
Et vous, Blanche la Savetiere,
Or est il temps de vous congnoistre.
Prenez a destre et a senestre;
N'espargnez homme, je vous prie:
Car vielles n'ont ne cours ne estre,
Ne que monnoye qu'on descrie.

« Et vous, la gente Saulciciere
Qui de dancier estre adestre,
Guillemete la Tapiciere,
Ne mesprenez vers vostre maistre:
Tost vous fauldra clorre fenestre;
Quant deviendrez vielle, flestrie,
Plus ne servirez qu'ung viel prestre,
Ne que monnoye qu'on descrie.

« Jehanneton la Chapperonniere,
Gardez qu'amy ne vous empestre;
Et Katherine la Bourciere,
N'envoyez plus les hommes paistre:
Car qui belle n'est, ne perpetre
Leur male grace, mais leur rie,
Laide viellesse amour n'empestre,
Ne que monnoye qu'on descrie.

« Filles, vueillez vous entremettre
D'escouter pourquoy pleure et crie:
Pour ce que je ne me puis mettre,
Ne que monnoye qu'on descrie. »

"This is how we complain
among ourselves, we poor old fools,
squatting on our haunches
in a heap like balls of wool,
by a little hemp-stalk fire, we—
aflame so young, so soon extinguished;
and to think we used to be so pretty!
But so it goes with one and all."   532

BALLADE*
(The Belle Hëaulmiere to the Daughters of Joy)

"So think things over, pretty Glover
who used to be my pupil,
and you, Blanche the Cobbler,
it's time you thought about yourself.
Take them right and left—spare no man
I pray you; for when you're old
you'll have less currency or place
than coins they've taken out of circulation.   540

"And you, sweet Sausage-vendor,
who's such a graceful dancer;
Guillemette the Tapestry-maker,
don't do your master in, for soon
you'll have to close your shop.
When you're old and faded
you'll be serving some old priest,
like coins they've taken out of circulation.   548

"Jeanneton the Bonnet-maker,
don't let your lover hobble you;
and Catherine, Purse-vendor,
stop putting men to pasture;
for even if those girls who aren't
so pretty, make no sour face, but smile,
old-age's ugliness will frighten love away,
like coins they've taken out of circulation.   556

"Girls, for your own good
listen to why I cry and weep:
I can no longer get around—I am
like coins they've taken out of circulation."   560

51

LVII Ceste leçon icy leur baille
La belle et bonne de jadis;
Bien dit ou mal, vaille que vaille,
Enregistrer j'ay faict ces dis
Par mon clerc Fremin[55] l'estourdis,
Aussi rassis que je pense estre.
S'il me desment, je le mauldis:
Selon le clerc est deu le maistre.

LVIII Si aperçoy le grant dangier
Ouquel homme amoureux se boute...
Et qui me vouldroit laidangier
De ce mot, en disant: « Escoute!
Se d'amer t'estrange et reboute
Le barat de celles nommees,
Tu fais une bien folle doubte,
Car ce sont femmes diffamees.

LIX « S'ilz n'ayment fors que pour l'argent,
On ne les ayme que pour l'eure;
Rondement ayment toute gent,
Et rient lors, quant bource pleure.
De celles cy n'est qui ne queure;
Mais en femmes d'onneur et nom
Franc homme, se Dieu me sequeure,
Se doit emploier; ailleurs, non. »

LX Je prens qu'aucun dye cecy,
Si ne me contente il en rien.
En effect il conclut ainsy,
Et je le cuide entendre bien,
Qu'on doit amer en lieu de bien:
Assavoir mon se ces filletes
Qu'en parolles toute jour tien
Ne furent ilz femmes honnestes?

LXI Honnestes si furent vraiement,
Sans avoir reproches ne blasmes.
Si est vray qu'au commencement
Une chascune de ces femmes
Lors prindrent, ains qu'eussent diffames,
L'une ung clerc, ung lay, l'autre ung moine.
Pour estaindre d'amours les flammes
Plus chauldes que feu saint Antoine.[56]

This lesson here is given them
by her who once was beautiful and good.
Well-said or not, whatever it is worth,
I've had these words put down
by my clerk, the scatterbrained Fremin,
who's about as sensible as I am.
I'll curse him if he contradicts me:
people judge the master by the clerk.*   568

I now see the great danger
a man in love encounters;
but some would doubtless want to blame me
for these words and say, "Listen!
If the deceits of those you mention
repel you and make you turn from love,
your fears indeed are foolish,
for these are women of ill repute.   576

"They love for money only, and in return
one loves them only for the moment;
they're not too fussy—they love everyone,
and laugh when purses weep.
Of these, there's none that's not a run-around;
but with women of honor and good name
(so help me God!) a decent man
should spend his time—with others, no."   584

When I imagine someone saying this,
it makes me quite unhappy.
In effect, this is his conclusion
(and I think I understand him),
that love must find a place of virtue.
But I'd like to know if these young girls
with whom I'm always chatting
weren't once as honest as the rest.   592

Yes, they once were really honest
—without reproach or blame.
It's true that when they started out
each one of them took on,
before they'd got their ill repute,
a clerk, a layman or a monk
to help put out love's flames—
a fire hotter than Saint Anthony's.*   600

53

LXII   Or firent selon le Decret[57]
Leurs amys, et bien y appert;
Ilz amoient en lieu secret,
Car autre d'eulx n'y avoit part.
Toutesfois, celle amour se part:
Car celle qui n'en avoit qu'un
De celuy s'eslongne et despart,
Et aime mieulx amer chascun.

LXIII   Qui les meut a ce? J'ymagine,
Sans l'onneur des dames blasmer,
Que c'est nature femenine
Qui tout vivement veult amer.
Autre chose n'y sçay rimer,
Fors qu'on dit a Rains et a Troys,
Voire a l'Isle et a Saint Omer,
Que six ouvriers[58] font plus que trois.

LXIV   Or ont ces folz amans le bont
Et les dames prins la vollee;
C'est le droit loyer qu'amans ont:
Toute foy y est viollee,
Quelque doulx baisier n'acollee.
« De chiens, d'oyseaulx, d'armes, d'amours, »
Chascun le dit a la vollee,
« Pour une joye cent doulours. »

DOUBLE BALLADE

Pour ce, amez tant que vouldrez,
Suyvez assemblees et festes,
En la fin ja mieulx n'en vauldrez
Et si n'y romprez que vos testes;
Folles amours font le gens bestes:
Salmon en ydolatria,
Samson en perdit ses lunetes.
Bien est eureux qui riens n'y a!

It's clear their lovers carried out
the words of the Decree:
they loved in secret—a love
in which no others had a part.
But this love soon was shared,
for she who only loves one man
gets bored, leaves him and acquires then
a taste for loving everyone.*   608

What makes them do this? I suppose,
without impugning women's honor,
that it's in their nature
to have such ardent need to love.
I know nothing else to tell,
except what's said at Reims or Troyes,
or even Lille or Saint-Omer, that six
workmen can do more than three.*   616

So these foolish lovers all get bounced—
their women leave them in the lurch;
this is the lover's recompense.
All faith is violated
however sweet the kisses and embraces.
"In riding to the hounds, in falconry,
in love or war," as anyone will tell you,
"for one brief joy a hundred woes."   624

DOUBLE BALLADE

So, have your fill of love,
go to parties and to banquets,
in the end you'll be no better off
and the only thing you'll break will be your head.
Foolish love makes beasts of men:
it once caused Solomon to worship idols,
and Samson to lose his eyes.
That man is lucky who has nothing.   632

Orpheüs, le doux menestrier,
Jouant de fleustes et musetes,
En fut en dangier d'un murtrier
Chien Cerberus a quatre testes;
Et Narcisus, le bel honnestes,
En ung parfont puis se noya
Pour l'amour de ses amouretes.[59]
Bien est eureux qui riens n'y a!

Sardana,[60] le preux chevalier,
Qui conquist le regne de Cretes,
En voulut devenir moullier
Et filler entre pucelletes;
David le roy, sage prophetes,
Crainte de Dieu en oublia,
Voyant laver cuisses bien faites.
Bien est eureux qui riens n'y a!

Amon en voult deshonnourer,
Faignant de menger tarteletes,
Sa seur Thamar et desflourer,
Qui fut inceste deshonnestes;
Herodes, pas ne sont sornetes,
Saint Jehan Baptiste en decola
Pour dances, saulx et chansonnetes.
Bien est eureux qui riens n'y a!

De moy, povre, je vueil parler:
J'en fus batu comme a ru telles,[61]
Tout nu, ja ne le quier celer.
Qui me feist maschier ces groselles,
Fors Katherine de Vausselles?
Noel, le tiers, est, qui fut la,
Mitaines a ces nopces telles.[62]
Bien est eureux qui riens n'y a!

Mais que ce jeune bacheler
Laissast ces jeunes bacheletes?
Non! et le deust on vif brusler
Comme ung chevaucheur d'escouvetes.[63]
Plus doulces luy sont que civetes;
Mais toutesfoys fol s'y fya:
Soient blanches, soient brunetes,
Bien est eureux qui riens n'y a!

Orpheus, the gentle minstrel,
playing flutes and bag-pipes,
because of love was at the mercy
of the four-headed dog, Cerberus;
and Narcissus, so fair and comely,
drowned himself in a deep well
because he loved so much to dally.
That man is lucky who has nothing.*   640

Sardana, the valiant knight
who conquered the kingdom of Crete,
wanted to become a woman
and spin flax among young girls;
David the King, wise prophet,
forgot his fear of God when he saw
smooth thighs being washed.
That man is lucky who has nothing.*   648

Love made Amnon wish to dishonor
(on a pretext of eating cakes)
his sister Tamar, and deflower her—
this was evil and incestuous;
and Herod (here there is no jesting)
had Saint John the Baptist's head cut off
for dances, jigs and little songs.
That man is lucky who has nothing.   656

I now must speak of my poor self: I, for love,
was thrashed like laundry by a stream,
stark naked—I no longer want to keep it quiet.
Who made me chew this bitter fruit
but Catherine de Vausselles?
Noël was also there—I hope he gets as badly
beaten up at his own wedding.
That man is lucky who has nothing.*   664

Is it possible that this young man
will leave young girls alone?
No—even were he burnt alive
like men that ride on brooms.
They're sweeter to him than civet-scent;
but all the same, a man is mad to trust them;
whether they're brunettes or blondes,
that man is lucky who has nothing.*   672

LXV   Se celle que jadis servoie
De si bon cuer et loyaument,
Dont tant de maulx et griefz j'avoie
Et souffroie tant de torment,
Se dit m'eust, au commencement,
Sa voulenté (mais nennil, las!)
J'eusse mis paine aucunement
De moy retraire de ses las.

LXVI   Quoy que je luy voulsisse dire,
Elle estoit preste d'escouter
Sans m'acorder ne contredire;
Qui plus, me souffroit acouter
Joignant d'elle, pres sacouter,
Et ainsi m'aloit amusant,
Et me souffroit tout raconter;
Mais ce n'estoit qu'en m'abusant.

LXVII   Abusé m'a et fait entendre
Tousjours d'ung que e fust ung aultre,
De farine que ce fust cendre,
D'ung mortier ung chappeau de faultre,
De viel machefer que fust peaultre,
D'ambesars que se fussent ternes,[64]
(Tousjours trompeur autruy enjaultre
Et rent vecies pour lanternes),

LXVIII   Du ciel une poille d'arain,
Des nues une peau de veau,
Du matin qu'estoit le serain,
D'ung trongnon de chou ung naveau,
D'orde cervoise vin nouveau,
D'une truie ung molin a vent
Et d'une hart ung escheveau,
D'ung gras abbé ung poursuyvant.

LXIX   Ainsi m'ont Amours abusé
Et pourmené de l'uys au pesle.
Je croy qu'homme n'est si rusé,
Fust fin comme argent de coepelle,
Qui n'y laissast linge, drappelle,
Mais qu'il fust ainsi manyé
Comme moy, qui partout m'appelle
L'amant remys et regnyé.

If she whom formerly I served
so willingly and loyally,
from whom I'got such grief and pain
and suffered so much torment,
had told me when I met her
what she wanted (alas, she never did)
I might have thought of some escape
from those nets she threw around me.   680

To whatever thing I wished to say
she listened willingly,
without assent or contradiction;
what's more, she let me get up close
to her and whisper in her ear.
She kept stringing me along like this
and let me open up my heart
—only to make fun of me.   688

She fooled me, making me believe
that one thing was another,
that flour was really ashes,
that a judge's hat was made of felt,
that old clinkers were really pewter,
that snake-eyes were big-Dicks,
(cheaters always fool the rest and make
them think the moon is made of cheese),*   696

the sky a copper pot,
clouds a hide of calf,
morning she said was evening dew,
a cabbage stump a turnip,
dirty barley-beer new wine,
a war-machine a windmill,
a hangman's noose a skein of yarn,
a paunchy abbot a herald's squire.   704

Thus has love abused me
and tossed me out the door.
I'm sure there's no man smart enough,
(were his wits as fine as purest silver),
to avoid being stripped by love
of his last rags and beaten just as I,
who everywhere am called
the rejected, discarded lover.   712

LXX   Je regnie Amours et despite
Et deffie a feu et a sang.
Mort par elles me precipite,
Et ne leur en chault pas d'ung blanc.
Ma vïelle ay mys soubz le banc;
Amans je ne suyvray jamais:
Se jadis je fus de leur ranc,
Je desclare que n'en suis mais.

LXXI   Car j'ay mys le plumail au vent,
Or le suyve qui a attente.
De ce me tais doresnavant,
Car poursuivre vueil mon entente.
Et s'aucun m'interroge ou tente
Comment d'Amours j'ose mesdire,
Ceste parolle le contente:
« Qui meurt, a ses loix de tout dire. »

LXXII   Je congnois approcher ma seuf;
Je crache, blanc comme coton,
Jacoppins gros comme ung esteuf.
Qu'esse a dire? que Jehanneton[65]
Plus ne me tient pour valeton,
Mais pour ung viel usé roquart:
De viel porte voix et le ton,
Et ne suys qu'ung jeune coquart.

LXXIII   Dieu mercy et Tacque Thibault,[66]
Qui tant d'eaue froide m'a fait boire,
Mis en bas lieu, non pas en hault,
Mengier d'angoisse mainte poire,
Enferré... Quant j'en ay memoire,
Je prie pour luy *et reliqua,*
Que Dieu luy doint, et voire, voire!
Ce que je pense... *et cetera.*

LXXIV   Toutesfois, je n'y pense mal
Pour lui et pour son lieutenant,[67]
Aussi pour son official,
Qui est plaisant et advenant;
Que faire n'ay du remenant,
Mais du petit maistre Robert.
Je les ayme, tout d'ung tenant,
Ainsi que fait Dieu le Lombart.

I renounce and curse all loves
and defy them with blood and fire.
They send me to my death
without a single thought.
So I've put away my fiddle; no longer
will I spend my time with lovers.
If I used to be among their ranks,
I swear I am no more.   720

I've put the feather to the wind
—follow it who may.
Now I'll drop this subject—I must get on
with what I started out to do.
If someone asks me or inquires
how I dare to speak such ill of love,
let this saying be enough:
"A dying man can speak his mind."   728

I feel my thirst approaching:
I spit gobs of phlegm as white
as cotton, as big as tennis balls.
What is there to say? That Jeanneton
no longer takes me for a youth,
but for an ancient, worn-out hack.
Already my voice is old and cracked,
and here I am still young and green.*   736

Thanks to God—and to Tacque Thibaud
who made me drink so much cold water,
put me underground instead of higher up
and made me eat such bitter fruit,
in chains. . . When I think of this,
I pray for him—*et reliqua*;
may God grant him (yes, by God)
what I think . . . *et cetera.**   744

Nevertheless, I bear him no
ill will, nor his lieutenant,
nor even his official
who's so pleasant and agreeable;
with the rest I have no doings,
except with little Master Robert.
I love them all as one—
as much as God loves Lombards.*   752

LXXV   Si me souvient bien, Dieu mercis,
Que je feis a mon partement
Certains laiz, l'an cinquante six,
Qu'aucuns, sans mon consentement,
Voulurent nommer Testament;
Leur plaisir fut, non pas le myen.
Mais quoy? on dit communement
Qu'ung chascun n'est maistre du sien.

LXXVI   Pour les revoquer ne le dis,
Et y courust toute ma terre;
De pitié ne suis refroidis
Envers le Bastart de la Barre:[68]
Parmi ses trois gluyons de fuerre
Je luy donne mes vieilles nates;
Bonnes seront pour tenir serre
Et soy soustenir sur les pates.

LXXVII   S'ainsi estoit qu'aucun n'eust pas
Receu le laiz que je luy mande,
J'ordonne qu'après mon trespas
A mes hoirs en face demande.
Mais qui sont ils? S'on le demande:
Moreau, Provins, Robin Turgis.[69]
De moy, dictes que je leur mande,
Ont eu jusqu'au lit ou je gis.

LXXVIII   Somme, plus ne diray qu'ung mot,
Car commencer vueil a tester:
Devant mon clerc Fremin[70] qui m'ot,
S'il ne dort, je vueil protester
Que n'entens homme detester
En ceste presente ordonnance,
Et ne la vueil magnifester
Si non ou royaume de France.

LXXIX   Je sens mon cuer qui s'affoiblit
Et plus je ne puis papier.
Fremin, sié toy pres de mon lit,
Que l'on ne me viengne espier;
Prens ancre tost, plume et papier;
Ce que nomme escry vistement,
Puys fay le partout coppier;
Et vecy le commancement.

I remember well, praise God,
that I composed on my departure
certain legacies, in 'fifty-six,
which some, with no consent of mine,
have wished to call a Testament;
the wish was theirs, not mine.
But so what? They say
no man is master of his own.   760

I don't say this to revoke them,
even though my lands were all at stake;
my pity towards the Bâtard
de la Barre has not been chilled;
along with his three bales of straw
I give him my old matting,
to help him hold on tight
and stay up on his feet.*   768

If someone did not receive
the legacy I gave him,
I command that after I am dead
he ask my heirs for it.
But who are they? If he should ask,
they're Moreau, Provins, Robin Turgis.
Say that my command is binding (from me
they even got the bed I sleep in).*   776

So, I won't say one more word,
for I must begin to make my will.
Before my clerk Fremin who's listening,
if he's not yet asleep, I want to state
that I intend to cut off no one
from my will in this new testament,
which I'd prefer were not made public,
except perhaps in France.*   784

I feel my heart grow feeble
and can hardly speak.
Fremin, sit near my bed
so people cannot spy on me.
Take pen and ink, and paper,
and write down quickly what I say,
then have it copied everywhere.
Here is the beginning: 792

LXXX   Ou nom de Dieu, Pere eternel,
        Et du Filz que vierge parit,
        Dieu au Pere coeternel,
        Ensemble et le Saint Esperit,
        Qui sauva ce qu'Adam perit
        Et du pery pare les cieulx ...
        Qui bien ce croit, peu ne merit,
        Gens mors estre faiz petiz dieux.

LXXXI   Mors estoient, et corps et ames,
        En dampnee perdicion,
        Corps pourris et ames en flammes,
        De quelconque condicion.
        Toutesfois, fais excepcion
        Des patriarches et prophetes;
        Car, selon ma concepcion,
        Oncques n'eurent grant chault aux fesses.

LXXXII   Qui me diroit: « Qui vous fait metre
        Si tres avant ceste parolle,
        Qui n'estes en theologie maistre?
        A vous est presumpcion folle. »
        C'est de Jhesus la parabolle[71]
        Touchant du Riche ensevely
        En feu, non pas en couche molle,
        Et du Ladre de dessus ly.

LXXXIII   Se du Ladre eust veu le doit ardre,
        Ja n'en eust requis refrigere,
        N'au bout d'icelluy doit aherdre
        Pour rafreschir sa maschouëre.
        Pyons y feront mate chiere,
        Qui boyvent pourpoint et chemise,
        Puis que boiture y est si chiere.
        Dieu nous en gart, bourde jus mise!

LXXXIV   Ou nom de Dieu, comme j'ay dit,
        Et de sa glorieuse Mere,
        Sans pechié soit parfait ce dit
        Par moy, plus megre que chimere;
        Se je n'ay eu fievre eufumere,
        Ce m'a fait divine clemence;
        Mais d'autre dueil et perte amere
        Je me tais, et ainsi commence.

In the name of God, eternal Father,
and of the Son, born of virgin,
God and Father coeternal
together with the Holy Ghost,
who saved what Adam lost
and adorns the heavens with the damned. . .
That man is worthy who believes
the dead are turned to saints.   800

They were dead in soul and body,
doomed forever to damnation,
their bodies rotten, their souls in flames,
no matter what had been their state before.
I make exception, though,
of all the patriarchs and prophets
who, as I see things,
never had their buttocks overheated.   808

Some, no doubt, will tell me: "How dare you,
who are no master of theology,
make such remarks as these.
Your presumption is a bit too much."
I would tell him this was Jesus'
parable about the rich man buried
in Hell's flames rather than a downy bed,
and Lazarus on high above him. *   816

Had he seen Lazarus' finger burning
he would not have asked to have it
cool him, nor to feel the water at its tip
refresh his burning throat.
Guzzlers who, since drinks are so expensive,
imbibe their coats and shirts
would not fare so well down there.
May God spare us this, all jokes aside.   824

In the name of God, as I have said,
and of His Glorious Mother,
may this work be finished without taint
of sin by me, who am more haggard than a ghost;
if I have had no cholera,
it's thanks to Heaven's clemency.
But of my other miseries and bitter loss
I now say nothing—and so begin.   832

LXXXV   Premier, je donne ma povre ame
A la benoiste Trinité,
Et la commande a Nostre Dame,
Chambre de la divinité,
Priant toute la charité
Des dignes neuf Ordres des cieulx[72]
Que par eulx soit ce don porté
Devant le Trosne precieux.

LXXXVI   Item, mon corps j'ordonne et laisse
A nostre grant mere la terre;
Les vers n'y trouveront grant gresse,
Trop luy a fait fain dure guerre.
Or luy soit delivré grant erre:
De terre vint, en terre tourne;
Toute chose, se par trop n'erre,
Voulentiers en son lieu retourne.

LXXXVII   Item, et a mon plus que pere,
Maistre Guillaume de Villon,[73]
Qui esté m'a plus doulx que mere
A enfant levé de maillon:
Degeté m'a de maint bouillon,
Et de cestuy pas ne s'esjoye,
Si luy requier a genouillon
Qu'il m'en laisse toute la joye;

LXXXVIII   Je luy donne ma librairie,
Et le Rommant du Pet au Deable,[74]
Lequel maistre Guy Tabarie
Grossa, qui est homs veritable.
Par cayers est soubz une table;
Combien qu'il soit rudement fait,
La matiere est si tres notable
Qu'elle amende tout le mesfait.

LXXXIX   Item, donne a ma povre mere
Pour saluer nostre Maistresse,
(Qui pour moy ot douleur amere,
Dieu le scet, et mainte tristesse),
Autre chastel n'ay, ne fortresse,
Ou me retraye corps ne ame,
Quant sur moy court malle destresse,
Ne ma mere, la povre femme!

First I give my poor soul
to the Blessed Trinity
and commend it to Our Lady,
chamber of Divinity,
praying that through the charity
of those nine worthy Orders
of Heaven, this gift be brought
before the precious Throne.*   840

Item: my body I bequeath and give
to our great mother earth;
the worms won't find much fat,
for hunger's waged too rude a war on it.
Let it be delivered soon:
from earth it came and to earth returns.
All things, unless they wander too far off,
willingly come back to their own place.   848

Item: to my more than father,
Master Guillaume de Villon,
who to me has been more tender than a mother
with a child removed from swaddling clothes;
he got me out of many scrapes,
but is none too happy over this one,
so on my knees I beg him
to leave this foul affair to me.*   856

I bequeath to him my library,
and the *Romance of the Devil's Fart*,
which Master Guy Tabary,
a very honest fellow, copied:
it's in notebooks beneath a table.
Even though it's not well written,
its subject is so notable
as to compensate for all defects.*   864

Item: I bequeath to my poor mother,
who for me bore bitter pain,
God knows, and many sorrows,
a salutation to Our Mistress—
I have no other house or fortress
in which to rest my soul and body
when some grim distress comes over me—
neither has my mother, poor old woman!   872

BALLADE
(pour prier Nostre Dame)

Dame du ciel, regente terrienne,
Emperiere des infernaux palus,
Recevez moy, vostre humble chrestienne,
Que comprinse soye entre vos esleus,
Ce non obstant qu'oncques rien ne valus.
Les biens de vous, ma Dame et ma Maistresse,
Sont trop plus grans que ne suis pecheresse,
Sans lesquelz biens ame ne peut merir
N'avoir les cieulx. Je n'en suis jangleresse:
En ceste foy je vueil vivre et mourir.

A vostre Filz dictes que je suis sienne;
De luy soyent mes pechiez abolus;
Pardonne moy comme a l'Egipcienne,
Ou comme il feist au clerc Theophilus,[75]
Lequel par vous fut quitte et absolus,
Combien qu'il eust au deable fait promesse.
Preservez moy que ne face jamais ce,
Vierge portant, sans rompture encourir,
Le sacrement qu'on celebre a la messe:
En ceste foy je vueil vivre et mourir.

Femme je suis povrette et ancïenne,
Qui riens ne sçay; oncques lettre ne lus.
Au moustier[76] voy dont suis paroissienne
Paradis paint, ou sont harpes et lus,
Et ung enfer ou dampnez sont boullus:
L'ung me fait paour, l'autre joye et liesse.
La joye avoir me fay, haulte Deesse,
A qui pecheurs doivent tous recourir,
Comblez de foy, sans fainte ne paresse:
En ceste foy je vueil vivre et mourir.

Vous portastes, digne Vierge, princesse,
Iesus regnant qui n'a ne fin ne cesse.
Le Tout Puissant, prenant nostre foiblesse,
Laissa les cieulx et nous vint secourir,
Offrit a mort sa tres chiere jeunesse;
Nostre Seigneur tel est, tel le confesse:
En ceste foy je vueil vivre et mourir.

BALLADE
(As a Prayer to Our Lady)

Lady of Heaven, Regent of earth,
Empress of the infernal marshes,
take me, your humble servant,
that I may be among your chosen people,
even though my worth has been as nothing.
Your mercy, my Lady and my Mistress,
is much greater than my sins—
without it no soul can be deserving
nor enter Heaven. Here I tell no lies:
in this faith I wish to live and die. 882

Tell your Son that I am His;
may he pardon me, and forgive my sins
as He did those of the Egyptian
or of the clerk Theophilus,
who was acquitted and absolved by you
though he had made a pact with Satan.
Preserve me from ever doing such a thing,
O Virgin who, undefiled, carried
the sacrament we celebrate at Mass.
In this faith I wish to live and die.* 892

I am a woman old, poor, and ignorant,
who has never learned to read.
In my parish church I see
a painted Paradise with harps and lutes
and a Hell where the damned are boiled:
one frightens me—the other gives me joy and happiness.
Let me have that joy, high Goddess,
to whom all sinners in the end must come,
filled with faith, without idleness or pretense.
In this faith I wish to live and die.* 902

You bore, worthy Virgin, Princess,
Jesus whose reign is without end.
He, all-powerful, taking on our feebleness,
left Heaven to come and save us,
and offered up His dearest youth to death.
He is our Lord; as such do I acknowledge Him.
In this faith I wish to live and die. 909

XC
Item, m'amour, ma chiere Rose,[77]
Ne luy laisse ne cuer ne foye;
Elle ameroit mieulx autre chose,
Combien qu'elle ait assez monnoye.
Quoy? une grant bource de soye,
Plaine d'escuz, parfonde et large;
Mais pendu soit il, que je soye,
Qui luy laira escu ne targe.[78]

XCI
Car elle en a, sans moy, assez.
Mais de cela il ne m'en chault;
Mes plus grans dueilz en sont passez,
Plus n'en ay le croppion chault.
Si m'en desmetz aux hoirs Michault,
Qui fut nommé le Bon Fouterre;[79]
Priez pour luy, faictes ung sault:
A Saint Satur gist, soubz Sancerre.

XCII
Ce non obstant, pour m'acquitter
Envers Amours, plus qu'envers elle,
Car onques n'y peuz acquester
D'espoir une seule estincelle
(Je ne sçay s'a tous si rebelle
A esté, ce m'est grant esmoy;
Mais, par sainte Marie la belle!
Je n'y voy que rire pour moy),

XCIII
Ceste ballade luy envoye
Qui se termine tout par R.
Qui luy portera? Que jo voye.
Ce sera Pernet de la Barre,[80]
Pourveu, s'il rencontre en son erre
Ma damoiselle au nez tortu,
Il luy dira, sans plus enquerre:
« Orde paillarde, dont viens tu? »

Item: to my love, my dearest Rose
neither heart nor faith I give;
she might prefer some other thing,
although the cash she has is quite enough.
Hm? Perhaps a big, silk purse,
deep, wide, and full of coins.
But I hope they hang the man (and me
included) who gives her any money.*   917

Even without me she's got enough,
but these things no longer bother me;
the worst of all my miseries are over
and my pants no longer hot.
I leave her to the heirs of that Michaud
they called the Fearless F———er;
pray for him and jump for joy—
he lies at Saint-Satur below Sancerre.*   925

However, to acquit myself toward Love,
rather than toward her,
for never would she give me
even one small ray of hope
(I don't know—and this still bothers me—
if she was so recalcitrant with everyone;
but by Saint Mary's beauty,
I now can finally laugh at this),   933

to her I send this ballade
with all the rhymes in R.
Who'll take it to her? Let me see.
Why not Perrenet de la Barre,
on condition that if he meets
my lady with the twisted nose,
he'll say to her, with no formalities:
"Where've you been, you filthy slut?"*   941

BALLADE[81]
(*a s'amye*)

Faulse beauté qui tant me couste chier,
Rude en effect, ypocrite doulceur,
Amour dure plus que fer a maschier,
Nommer que puis, de ma desfaçon seur,
Cherme felon, la mort d'ung povre cuer,
Orgueil mussié qui gens met au mourir,
Yeulx sans pitié, ne veult Droit de Rigueur,
Sans empirer, ung povre secourir?

Mieulx m'eust valu avoir esté serchier
Ailleurs secours: c'eust esté mon onneur;
Riens ne m'eust sceu lors de 'ce fait hachier.
Trotter m'en fault en fuyte et deshonneur.
Haro, haro, le grant et le mineur!
Et qu'esse cy? Mourray sans coup ferir?
Ou Pitié veult, selon ceste teneur,
Sans empirer, ung povre secourir?

Vng temps viendra qui fera dessechier,
Jaunir, flestrir vostre espanye fleur;
Je m'en risse, se tant peusse maschier
Lors; mais nennil, ce seroit donc foleur:
Viel je seray; vous, laide, sans couleur;
Or beuvez fort, tant que ru peut courir;
Ne donnez pas a tous ceste douleur,
Sans empirer, ung povre secourir.

Prince amoureux, des amans le greigneur,
Vostre mal gré ne vouldroye encourir,
Mais tout franc cuer doit par Nostre Seigneur,
Sans empirer, ung povre secourir.

XCIV   Item, a maistre Ythier Marchant,
Auquel mon branc laissai jadis,
Donne, mais qu'il le mette en chant,
Ce lay contenant des vers dix,
Et, au luz, ung *De profundis*
Pour ses ancïennes amours
Desquelles le nom je ne dis,
Car il me hairoit a tous jours.

BALLADE*
(*To his Girl Friend*)

False beauty, for which I pay so great a price,
harsh behind a mask of sweetness and hypocrisy,
a love that's tougher on the teeth than steel
and surely harbinger of my undoing,
felon charm, death of my poor heart,˙
secret pride which sends men to their destruction,
eyes which have no pity, will not justice
help a poor man without crushing him?   949

I would have done much better seeking help
some other place; my honor would have been unscathed.
No other lure would then have tempted me,
but now I must retreat in shame.
Help me, help me, anyone!
But what? I'll die and not get in one blow?
Or will Pity, moved by these sad words
help a poor man without crushing him?   957

A time will come when your flower, now in bloom,
will dry up, wilt and turn yellow;
then I'll laugh, if I still can move my jaws;
but no, that would be madness:
I'll be old, you ugly and without color.
So drink deep before the stream runs dry;
don't bring down this misery on everyone—
help a poor man without crushing him.   965

Prince of lovers, greatest of them all,
I wouldn't like to bring on your disfavor,
but, by Our Lord, all noble hearts must
help a poor man without crushing him.   969

Item: to Master Ythier Marchand
to whom I left my sword before,
I now bequeath ten lines of verse
which he must set for voice,
and for the lute, a *De Profundis*
for his old loves, whose names
I will not mention, or otherwise
he would forever hate me.   977

LAY[82]
(*Rondeau*)

Mort, j'appelle de ta rigueur,
Qui m'as ma maistresse ravie,
Et n'es pas encore assouvie
Se tu ne me tiens en langueur.

Oncques puis n'eus force, vigueur;
Mais que te nuysoit elle en vie?
Mort, j'appelle de ta rigueur,
Qui m'as ma maistresse ravie.

Deux estions et n'avions qu'ung cuer;
S'il est mort, force est que devie,
Voire, ou que je vive sans vie
Comme les images, par cuer.

XCV   Item, a maistre Jehan Cornu[83]
Autre nouveau laiz lui vueil faire,
Car il m'a tous jours secouru
A mon grant besoing et affaire;
Pour ce, le jardin luy transfere,
Que maistre Pierre Bobignon
M'arenta, en faisant refaire
L'uys et redrecier le pignon.

XCVI   Par faulte d'ung uys, j'y perdis
Ung grez et ung manche de houe.
Alors huit faulcons, non pas dix,
N'y eussent pas prins une aloue.
L'ostel est seur, mais qu'on le cloue.
Pour enseigne y mis ung havet;
Qui que l'ait prins, point ne m'en loue:
Sanglante nuyt et bas chevet!

XCVII   Item, et pour ce que la femme
De maistre Pierre Saint Amant[84]
(Combien, se coulpe y a a l'ame,
Dieu luy pardonne doulcement!)
Me mist ou renc de cayement,
Pour *le Cheval Blanc* qui ne bouge
Luy change a une jument,
Et *la Mulle* a ung asne rouge.

LAY*
(*Rondeau*)

Death, I appeal against your harshness
which took away my mistress,
and still you'll not be satisfied
until you have me listless too.   981

Since then, I've had no strength or vigor.
But when alive, what harm did she do you?
Death, I appeal against your harshness
which took away my mistress.   985

We were two, but only had one heart;
if it is dead, I too must pass away—
yes, or live entirely lifeless
like an image carved in stone.   989

Item: to Master Jean Cornu
I'd like to make another legacy,
for he has always helped me through
my times of greatest need and trouble;
therefore, to him I transfer the garden
which Master Pierre Baubignon
rented me, and I'll have them put
the door back up and fix the gable.*   997

Because it lacked a door, I lost
in there a paving-stone and the handle
of a hoe. Eight falcons, or even ten,
could not have caught a lark in there.
The house is safe, but must be shut.
As a sign I hung a hook up there—
whoever took it, I hope he spends a goddamn
awful night stretched out on the ground.   1005

Item: and since the wife of Master
Pierre Saint-Amand
(if her soul bears blame for this,
may God gently grant her pardon!)
reduced me to the rank of beggar,
to the *White Horse* which won't budge
in exchange I give a mare,
and to the *She-Mule* a red-hot ass.*   1013

75

XCVIII   Item, donne a sire Denis
Hesselin,[85] esleu de Paris,
Quatorze muys de vin d'Aulnis
Prins sur Turgis a mes perilz.
S'il en buvoit tant que peris
En fust son sens et sa raison,
Qu'on mette de l'eaue es barilz:
Vin pert mainte bonne maison.

XCIX   Item, donne a mon advocat,
Maistre Guillaume Charruau,[86]
(Quoy que Marchant ot pour estat)
Mon branc; je me tais du fourreau.
Il aura avec ce ung reau
En change, affin que sa bource enfle,
Prins sur la chaussee et carreau
De la grant cousture du Temple.

C   Item, mon procureur Fournier[87]
Aura pour toutes ses corvees
(Simple sera de l'espargnier)
En ma bource quatre havees,
Car maintes causes m'a sauvees,
Justes, ainsi Jhesu Christ m'aide!
Comme telles se sont trouvees;
Mais bon droit a bon mestier d'aide.

CI   Item, je donne a maistre Jaques
Raguier[88] *le Grant Godet* de Greve,
Pourveu qu'il paiera quatre plaques,
(Deust il vendre, quoy qu'il luy griefve,
Ce dont on cueuvre mol et greve,
Aller sans chausses, en eschappin),
Se sans moy boit, assiet ne lieve,
Au trou de *la Pomme de Pin.*

CII   Item, quant est de Merebeuf
Et de Nicolas de Louviers,[89]
Vache ne leur donne ne beuf,
Car vachiers ne sont ne bouviers,
Mais gens a porter espreviers,
Ne cuidez pas que je me joue,
Et pour prendre perdris, plouviers,
Sans faillir, sur la Machecoue.

Item: I give to Sire Denis
Hesselin, Elect of Paris,
fourteen hogsheads of Aulnis wine,
taken from Turgis and charged to me.
Should he drink so much
that he obliterates his sense of reason,
then fill the barrels up with water:
many a decent house is lost through wine.*   1021

Item: I give my lawyer,
Master Guillaume Charruau
(even though I gave it to Marchand),
my sword. . . I'll keep mum about the sheath.
He'll get with this a *reau*
in change, to fatten up his purse,
picked up somewhere on the pavement
of the Templars' great domain.*   1029

Item: my advocate Fournier,
for all the thankless jobs he's done,
(such a sum could easily be saved)
shall have four fists-full from my purse,
for he has won me many cases,
and just ones too, by Jesus Christ!
As such they were decided; but a man
who's right must still have help.*   1037

Item: I bequeath to Master Jacques Raguier
The *Great Wine Cup* in the Place de Grève
as long as he will pay four *placques*
(even if he's forced, as painful as it is,
to sell what covers calf and thigh
and go bare-legged, wearing only slippers),
if he won't drink or lift a fork
with me at the *Pine-Cone* Tavern.*   1045

Item: as for Merbeuf
and Nicolas de Louviers,
I leave them neither bull nor cow
for they're no good as cattlemen,
but rather men to carry falcons
(don't think this is a joke)
to capture partridges and plovers
without fail from Madame Machecoue.*   1053

CIII   Item, viengne Robin Turgis[90]
A moy, je luy paieray son vin;
Combien, s'il treuve mon logis,
Plus fort sera que le devin.
Le droit luy donne d'eschevin,
Que j'ay comme enfant de Paris:
Se je parle ung peu poictevin,
Ice m'ont deux dames apris.

CIV   Elles sont tres belles et gentes,
Demourans a Saint Generou
Pres Saint Julien de Voventes,
Marche de Bretaigne a Poictou.
Mais i ne di proprement ou
Yquelles passent tous les jours;
M'arme! i ne seu mie si fou,
Car i vueil celer mes amours.

CV   Item, a Jehan Raguier[91] je donne,
Qui est sergent, voire des Douze,
Tant qu'il vivra, ainsi l'ordonne,
Tous les jours une tallemouse,
Pour bouter et fourrer sa mouse,
Prinse a la table de Bailly;
A Maubué sa gorge arrouse,
Car au mengier n'a pas failly.

CVI   Item, et au Prince des Sotz[92]
Pour ung bon sot Michault du Four,
Qui a la fois dit de bons motz
Et chante bien « Ma doulce amour! »
Je lui donne avec le bonjour;
Brief, mais qu'il fust ung peu en point,
Il est ung droit sot de sejour,
Et est plaisant ou il n'est point.

CVII   Item, aux Unze Vingtz Sergens[93]
Donne, car leur fait est honneste
Et sont bonnes et doulces gens,
Denis Richier et Jehan Vallette,
A chascun une grant cornete
Pour pendre a leurs chappeaulx de faultres;
J'entens a ceulx a pié, hohete!
Car je n'ay que faire des autres.

Item: should Robin Turgis come
to me, I'll pay him for his wine;
but if he finds out where I live,
he's sharper than a fortune-teller.
I'll give him the right of magistrate
I have being born in Paris;
if I speak a little southern dialect,
it's because two women taught me.*   1061

They're charming, and both pretty;
they live at Saint-Generoux
near Saint-Julien-de-Vouvantes
on the border of Poitou and Brittany.
*But ah ain't lettin no one in
on wheah these ladies spend theah time;
by Gawd, ah ain't so cracked as not
to button up mah lip about mah wimmin.*   1069

Item: I give to Jean Raguier,
who is a sergeant of the Twelve,
for as long as he may live
each day a cheese soufflé
(to be taken from Bailly's table)
to stuff into his mug. Then let him go
to the Maubué pump to wet his whistle,
for he'll have eaten quite enough.*   1077

Item: to the Prince of Fools I give
as aide Michault du Four, another fool,
who sometimes cracks good jokes
and sings "My Sweetest Love" quite well;
along with this I give him a "hello."
I hope that he improves a bit—
he's fairly foolish where he is,
but funny only where he isn't.*   1085

Item: among the Two Hundred Twenty Sergeants,
because they are so honest, and such
good and gentle people, I give
Denis Richier and Jean Valette
a velvet band to each
to hang from their felt hats;
I mean the ones on foot, of course—
I've had no doings with the others.*   1093

CVIII De rechief donne a Perrenet,
J'entens le Bastart de la Barre,[94]
Pour ce qu'il est beau filz et net,
En son escu, en lieu de barre,
Trois dez plombez, de bonne carre,
Et ung beau joly jeu de cartes.
Mais quoy? s'on l'oyt vecir ne poirre,
En oultre aura les fievres quartes.

CIX Item, ne vueil plus que Cholet[95]
Dolle, tranche, douve ne boise,
Relie broc ne tonnelet,
Mais tous ses houstilz changier voise
A une espee lyonnoise,
Et retiengne le hutinet;
Combien qu'il n'ayme bruyet ne noise,
Si luy plaist il ung tantinet.

CX Item, je donne a Jehan le Lou,[95]
Homme de bien et bon marchant,
Pour ce qu'il est linget et flou,
Et que Cholet est mal serchant,
Ung beau petit chiennet couchant
Qui ne laira poullaille en voye,
Ung long tabart et bien cachant
Pour les mussier, qu'on ne les voye.

CXI Item, a l'Orfevre de Bois,[96]
Donne cent clouz, queues et testes,
De gingembre sarrazinois,
Non pas pour accomplir ses boetes,
Mais pour conjoindre culz et coetes,
Et couldre jambons et andoulles,
Tant que le lait en monte aux tetes
Et le sang en devalle aux coulles.

CXII Au cappitaine Jehain Riou,[97]
Tant pour luy que pour ses archiers,
Je donne six hures de lou,
Qui n'est pas viande a porchiers,
Prinses a gros mastins de bouchiers,
Et cuites en vin de buffet.
Pour mengier de ces morceaulx chiers,
On en feroit bien ung malfait.

Once again I give to Perrenet,
I mean the Bastard de la Barre,
because he's such a clean-cut fellow,
for his escutcheon, instead of that
bar sinister, three loaded dice
and a fine new deck of cards.
What else? If someone hears him fart,
I hope he gets the quartan fever too.*   1101

Item: I'd prefer if Cholet would no longer
shave, saw, fashion staves, do carpentry,
or patch up jugs and casks,
but rather toss out all his tools
and change them for a Lyons sword,
but keep the mallet of his trade;
I'm not so sure he dislikes noise and racket
quite as much as he pretends.*   1109

Item: I give to Jean the Wolf,
a splendid man and A-1 merchant,
because he's thin and skinny
and because Cholet is such a rotten
hunter, a fine, small setter
who'll let no poultry pass him by,
and a cloak to hide things in
and stash these chickens out of sight.*   1117

Item: to The Woodsmith I bequeath
a hundred cloves of Moslem ginger,
complete with stems and heads,
not just to put in jars,
but to join together tails and arses
and sew up thighs and eels—
so much that milk makes nipples swell
and blood descends to testicles.*   1125

And to the Captain, Jean Riou,
as much for him as for his archers,
I give the meat from six wolves' heads
(which is no food for swine-herds),
snatched from butchers' dogs
and cooked in lousy, sour wine.
For tasty morsels such as these
a man would go to any lengths.*   1133

CXIII C'est vïande ung peu plus pesante
Que duvet n'est, plume, ne liege.
Elle est bonne a porter en tente,
Ou pour user en quelque siege.
S'ilz estoient prins a un piege,
Que ces mastins ne sceussent courre,
J'ordonne, moy qui suis son miege,
Que des peaulx, sur l'iver, se fourre.

CXIV Item, a Robinet Trascaille,[98]
Qui en service (c'est bien fait)
A pié ne va comme une caille,
Mais sur roncin gras et reffait,
Je lui donne, de mon buffet,
Une jatte qu'emprunter n'ose;
Si aura mesnage parfait:
Plus ne luy failloit autre chose.

CXV Item, donne a Perrot Girart,[99]
Barbier juré du Bourg la Royne,
Deux bacins et ung coquemart,
Puis qu'a gaignier met telle paine.
Des ans y a demie douzaine
Qu'en son hostel de cochons gras
M'apatella une sepmaine,
Tesmoing l'abesse de Pourras.

CXVI Item, aux Freres mendians,[100]
Aux Devotes et aux Beguines,
Tant de Paris que d'Orleans,
Tant Turlupins que Turlupines,
De grasses souppes jacoppines
Et flans leur fais oblacion;
Et puis après, soubz ces courtines,
Parler de contemplacion.

CXVII Si ne suis je pas qui leur donne,
Mais de tous enffans sont les meres,
Et Dieu, qui ainsi les guerdonne,
Pour qui seuffrent paines ameres.
Il faut qu'ilz vivent, les beaulx peres,[101]
Et mesmement ceulx de Paris.
S'ilz font plaisir a nos commeres,
Ilz ayment ainsi leurs maris.

Such meat is maybe somewhat heavier
than feathers, down or cork.
It's good for soldiers in the field
or for use in sieges.
If those wolves were caught in traps
and those dogs no good as hunters,
I, who am his doctor, command he use
their furs to line his coat in winter.   1141

Item: to Robinet Trascaille
who on his job (he does quite well)
never walks about as would a quail
but rides a fat and well-fed horse,
I give from among my pots and pans
a bowl which he has been too shy to borrow;
his household then will be complete
—he won't be lacking anything.*   1149

Item: I give Perrot Girart,
sworn barber of Bourg-la-Reine,
two basins and a kettle, because he works
so hard to make a living.
In his house a half a dozen
years ago he fed me on fat pork
for one whole week—the Abbess of Pourras
will bear me witness.*   1157

Item: to the Mendicants,
Filles-Dieu and Beguines
of Paris or from Orléans,
to male or female Turlupins
I make oblation of nice thick
Jacobin soups and custards;
then afterwards behind bed-curtains
they can speak of contemplation.*   1165

It's not I who gives them contributions,
but every mother of every child,
and God, who thus gives recompense
for these who suffer bitter pains.
They have to live, these handsome
fathers, and likewise those in Paris.
They keep our married women happy
and thereby prove their love to husbands.*   1173

CXVIII   Quoy que maistre Jehan de Poullieu[102]
En voulsist dire *et reliqua*,
Contraint et en publique lieu,
Honteusement s'en revoqua.
Maistre Jehan de Mehun s'en moqua
De leur façon, si fist Mathieu;
Mais on doit honnorer ce qu'a
Honnoré l'Eglise de Dieu.

CXIX   Si me soubmectz, leur serviteur
En tout ce que puis faire et dire,
A les honnorer de bon cuer
Et obeïr, sans contredire;
L'homme bien fol est d'en mesdire,
Car, soit a part ou en preschier
Ou ailleurs, il ne fault pas dire
Ses gens sont pour eux revenchier.

CXX   Item, je donne a frere Baude,[103]
Demourant en l'ostel des Carmes,
Portant chiere hardie et baude,
Une sallade et deux guysarmes,
Que de Tusca et ses gens d'armes
Ne lui riblent sa caige vert.
Viel est: s'il ne se rent aux armes,
C'est bien le deable de Vauvert.

CXXI   Item, pour ce que le Scelleur
Maint estront de mouche a maschié,[104]
Donne, car homme est de valeur,
Son seau d'avantage crachié,
Et qu'il ait le poulce escachié,
Pour tout empreindre a une voye;
J'entens celuy de l'Eveschié,
Car les autres, Dieu les pourvoye!

CXXII   Quant des auditeurs messeigneurs,[105]
Leur granche ilz auront lambroissee;
Et ceulx qui ont les culz rongneux,
Chascun une chaire percee;
Mais qu'a la petite Macee
D'Orleans, qui ot ma sainture,
L'amende soit bien hault tauxee:
Elle est une mauvaise ordure.

No matter what it was that Jean de Poullieu
wished to say against the friars,
they forced him to retract
his words in public.
Master Jean de Meung made fun of them,
and so did Matheolus;
but we must honor everything
that's honored by the Church of God.*   1181

So I, their servant, submit myself
in all that I may do or say
to honor them with open heart,
and to obey without a word against them;
a man is mad to curse them.
It's better to keep mum, for,
in private or from the pulpit,
they're masters at the art of self-defense.   1189

Item: I bequeath to Brother Baude,
a tough old bird who lives
among the Carmelites,
a helmet and two halberds
so de Tusca and his men-at-arms
won't snatch his little playmate.
He's old and if he doesn't soon put down
his arms, there might be Hell to pay.*   1197

Item: since the Keeper of the Seal
has had to chew on so much bee-dung
and because he's such a worthy man, I give
to him a seal with spit put on beforehand,
and may his thumb be squashed so he
can press the whole thing down at once.
I'm talking of the Bishop's clerk—
let God take care of all the rest.*   1205

As for Milords the Auditors,
they'll have their barn fixed up with panels,
and those who suffer from the piles
will have some chairs with holes in them.
But as for little Macée of Orléans
who has my money-belt,
let them slap a heavy fine on her
—she's nothing but a little slut.*   1213

CXXIII   Item, donne a maistre Françoys,
          Promoteur, de la Vacquerie[106]
          Ung hault gorgerin d'Escossoys,
          Toutesfois sans orfaverie;
          Car, quant receut chevallerie,
          Il maugrea Dieu et saint George:
          Parler n'en oit qui ne s'en rie,
          Comme enragié, a plaine gorge.

CXXIV   Item, a maistre Jehan Laurens,[107]
          Qui a les povres yeulx si rouges
          Pour le pechié de ses parens
          Qui boivent en baris et courges,
          Je donne l'envers de mes bouges
          Pour tous les matins les torchier;
          S'il fust arcevesque de Bourges,
          Du sendail eust, mais il est chier.

CXXV   Item, a maistre Jehan Cotart,[108]
          Mon procureur en court d'Eglise,
          Devoye environ ung patart,
          (Car a present bien m'en advise)
          Quant chicaner me feist Denise,
          Disant que l'avoye mauldite;
          Pour son ame, qu'es cieulx soit mise,
          Ceste oroison j'ai cy escripte.

BALLADE
(*et·oroison*)

Pere Noé, qui plantastes la vigne,[109]
Vous aussi, Loth, qui beustes ou rochier,
Par tel party qu'Amours, qui gens engigne,
De voz filles si vous feist approuchier
(Pas ne le dy pour le vous reprouchier),
Archetriclin, qui bien sceustes cest art,
Tous trois vous pry que vous vueillez pescher
L'ame du bon feu maistre Jehan Cotart!

Jadis extraict il fut de vostre ligne,
Luy qui buvoit du meilleur et plus chier,
Et ne deust il avoir vaillant ung pigne;
Certes, sur tous, c'estoit ung bon archier;
On ne luy sceut pot des mains arrachier;

86

Item: I bequeath to François
de la Vacquerie, attorney,
a Scottish throat-piece
without adornment;
for when they dubbed him knight,
he swore by God and by Saint George:
every one who heard about it laughed
until they thought their sides would split.*   1221

Item: to Master Jean Laurens,
who has such poor red eyes
because he has his parents' sin
of drinking out of pails and barrels,
I bequeath my suit-case linings
to wipe them every morning.
Were he Archbishop of a town like Bourges
he might use silk—but it's expensive.*   1229

Item: to Master Jean Cotart,
my lawyer in the Court of Church,
I owed a penny (I now remember)
from when Denise
brought me before the law
because of my abusive language;
for his soul (may it be put in Heaven)
I've composed this prayer:*   1237

BALLADE
(and Prayer)

Father Noah who planted the vine,
you too, Lot, who drank in the cave
until Love, who makes fools out of men,
made you lie with your daughters
(I don't say this to reproach you),
Architriclinus, well versed in this art,
all three, I pray you to save
the soul of the late Master Jean Cotart.*   1245

He used to be one of your lineage,
he who drank only the best and the dearest
without a red cent to his name.
Yes, this man was the finest of guzzlers;
no one could make him let go of his mug—

De bien boire ne fut oncques fetart.
Nobles seigneurs, ne souffrez empeschier
L'ame du bon feu maistre Jehan Cotart!

Comme homme beu qui chancelle et trepigne
L'ay veu souvent, quant il s'alloit couchier,
Et une fois il se feist une bigne,
Bien m'en souvient, a l'estal d'ung bouchier
Brief, on n'eust sceu en ce monde serchier
Meilleur pyon, pour boire tost et tart.
Faictes entrer quant vous orrcz huchier
L'ame du bon feu maistre Jehan Cotart!

Prince, il n'eust sceu jusqu'a terre crachier;
Tousjours crioit: « Haro! la gorge m'art. »
Et si ne sceust oncq sa seuf estanchier
L'ame du bon feu maistre Jehan Cotart.

CXXVI Item, vueil que le jeune Merle[110]
Desormais gouverne mon change,
Car de changier envys me mesle,
Pourveu que tousjours baille en change,
Soit a privé soit a estrange,
Pour trois escus six brettes targes,
Pour deux angelotz ung grant ange:
Car amans doivent estre larges.

CXXVII Item, j'ay sceu en ce voyage
Que mes trois povres orphelins[111]
Sont creus et deviennent en aage
Et n'ont pas testes de belins,
Et qu'enfans d'icy a Salins
N'a mieulx sachans leur tour d'escolle.
Or, par l'ordre des Mathelins,
Telle jeunesse n'est pas folle.

CXXVIII Si vueil qu'ilz voisent a l'estude;
Ou? sur maistre Pierre Richier.[112]
Le Donat est pour eulx trop rude:
Ja ne les y vueil empeschier,
Ilz sauront, je l'ayme plus chier,
Ave salus, tibi decus,
Sans plus grans lettres enserchier:
Tousjours n'ont pas clers l'au dessus.

he never was lazy in this business of drinking.
Noble Lords, allow no impediments in the way
of the soul of the late Master Jean Cotart.   1253

Like a drunkard, staggering and reeling,
I often have seen him as he went off to bed,
and once, I remember, he got his head
bruised on a butcher's stall. In short,
in all the wide world one could not find
a lush who was better to drink with day or night.
So, when you hear someone cry, open the gates
for the soul of the late Master Jean Cotart.   1261

Prince, he scarcely could spit on the ground:
he always would shout, "Help! My throat is on fire!",
and it never could quench its thirst,
the soul of the late Master Jean Cotart.   1265

Item: I would like young Merle
to take over my money-changing
(which I do against my will)
on one condition: both to friends
and strangers he must exchange
six Breton *targes* for three *écus*,
and an angel for two angelets—
for lovers should be generous. *   1273

Item: I found out, while traveling,
that my three poor orphans
have grown up, become of age,
and are no mutton-heads,
and that no kids from here to Salins
have learnt their lessons better.
So, by the Order of the Mathurins,
a youth like that is not ill-spent. *   1281

My will is that they study.
Where? With Master Pierre Richier.
The *Donatus* is too tough for them,
and I'd prefer them not to get bogged down.
Better they should know
the *Ave salus, tibi decus*,
and not try for higher learning;
scholars do not always come out best. *   1289

CXXIX   Cecy estudient, et ho!
Plus proceder je leur deffens.
Quant d'entendre le grant *Credo*,[113]
Trop forte elle est pour telz enfans.
Mon long tabart en deux je fens;
Si vueil que la moitié s'en vende
Pour eulx en acheter des flans,
Car jeunesse est ung peu friande.

CXXX   Et vueil qu'ilz soient informez
En meurs, quoy que couste bature;
Chaperons auront enformez
Et les poulces sur la sainture,[114]
Humbles a toute creature,
Disans: « Han? Quoy? Il n'en est rien! »
Si diront gens, par adventure:
« Vecy enfans de lieu de bien! »

CXXXI   Item, et mes povres clerjons,[115]
Auxquelz mes tiltres resigné:
Beaulx enfans et droiz comme jons
Les voyant, m'en dessaisiné,
Cens recevoir leui assigné,
Seur comme qui l'auroit en paulme,
A ung certain jour consigné,
Sur l'ostel de Gueuldry Guillaume.

CXXXII   Quoy que jeunes et esbatans
Soient, en riens ne me desplaist:
Dedens trente ans ou quarante ans
Bien autres seront, se Dieu plaist.
Il fait mal qui ne leur complaist,
Ilz sont tres beaulx enfans et gens;
Et qui les bat ne fiert, fol est,
Car enfans si deviennent gens.

CXXXIII   Les bources des Dix et Huit Clers[116]
Auront; je m'y vueil travaillier:
Pas ilz ne dorment comme loirs
Qui trois mois sont sans resveillier.
Au fort, triste est le sommeillier
Qui fait aisier jeune en jeunesse
Tant qu'en fin lui faille veillier,
Quant reposer deust en viellesse.

They'll study this—then whoa!
I forbid them to go further.
As for understanding the great *Credo*,
that's too much for such small children.
I'll tear in two my long coat;
let half of it be sold, so they
can buy themselves some custards,
for youth is fond of sweets.*   1297

I also will that they be taught
good manners even if they must be flogged;
their hoods must be on tight
and their thumbs stuck in their belts,
and to everyone they must be humble
and say, "Hm? What? Don't mention it."
Thus, perhaps, will people say of them:
"Now there are well-bred children."*   1305

Item: those poor young clerks
to whom I made my titles over
because they were such handsome kids
and stood as straight as ramrods,
I assigned to them that rent
(which was as good as in their hands:
it was arranged one day in court)
from Guillaume Gueldry's house.*   1313

Even though they're young and love
to play, I don't at all dislike them;
within some thirty or forty years
they'll be quite changed, God willing.
It would be wrong for someone not to treat
them nicely, these lovely gentle boys;
who beats or strikes them must be mad,
for children will be people later on.   1321

They'll have the pension of the Eighteen
Clerk's; I'll see to that myself.
They don't sleep like doormice
who go three months without awakening.
Yes, it's sad, this sleep in which
the young find pleasure in their youth,
until they're forced to stay awake instead
of resting as they should in their old age.*   1329

CXXXIV Sy en rescriptz au collateur[117]
Lettres semblables et pareilles:
Or prient pour leur bienfaicteur,
Ou qu'on leur tire les oreilles.
Aucunes gens ont grans merveilles
Que tant m'encline vers ces deux;
Mais, foy que doy festes et veilles,
Oncques ne vy les meres d'eulx!

CXXXV Item, donne a Michault Cul d'Oue[118]
Et a sire Charlot Taranne
Cent solz (s'ilz demandent: « Prins ou? »
Ne leur chaille; ilz vendront de manne)
Et unes houses de basanne,
Autant empeigne que semelle,
Pourveu qu'ilz me salueront Jehanne,
Et autant une autre comme elle.

CXXXVI Item, au seigneur de Grigny,[119]
Auquel jadis laissay Vicestre,
Je donne la tour de Billy
Pourveu, s'uys y a ne fenestre
Qui soit ne debout ne en estre,
Qu'il mette tres bien tout a point.
Face argent a destre et senestre:
Il m'en fault et il n'en a point.

CXXXVII Item, a Thibault de la Garde...
Thibault? je mens, il a nom Jehan;[120]
Que luy donray je, que ne perde?
(Assez ay perdu tout cest an;
Dieu y vueille pourveoir, *amen*!)
Le Barillet, par m'ame, voire!
Genevoys est plus ancïen
Et a plus beau nez pour y boire.

CXXXVIII Item, je donne a Basennier,[121]
Notaire et greffier criminel,
De giroffle plain ung pannier
Prins sur maistre Jehan de Ruel,
Tant a Mautaint, tant a Rosnel,
Et, avec ce don de giroffle,
Servir de cuer gent et ysnel
Le seigneur qui sert saint Cristofle,

And letters just like these
I'll write to the collator;
let them pray for me their benefactor;
if not, let someone yank their ears.
Some people seem surprised
at all my fondness for these two;
but on my honor, in any feast or fast,
I've never seen their mothers.*   1337

Item: I give to Michault Culdoe
and Sire Charlot Taranne a hundred *sous*
(if they ask, "Where from?", they
shouldn't worry—it'll fall like manna),
and a pair of sheepskin boots
complete with tops and soles,
provided they go visit Jeanne
and another just like her.*   1345

Item: to the Lord of Grigny,
to whom I left Bicêtre before,
I now give the Billy Tower,
provided, if there are no doors or windows
still in place and functioning,
he fix up everything.
Let money rain to left and right;
I need some—and he has none.*   1353

Item: to Thibaud de la Garde. . .
Thibaud? I lie—his name is Jean.
What'll I give that won't involve a loss
for me? (I've lost enough this year;
may God repair my needs—Amen!)
The Keg, by Christ—that's it!
But Genevois is older and has a finer
redder nose to drink from it.*   1361

Item: I give to Basanier,
criminal clerk and notary,
a basket full of cloves, which he
shall take from Master Jean de Rueil,
and the same to Mautaint and Rosnel;
and with this gift of cloves, I command
they serve with prompt and humble heart
the lord devoted to Saint Christopher,*   1369

93

CXXXIX Auquel ceste ballade donne
Pour sa dame, qui tous biens a;
S'Amour ainsi tous ne guerdonne,
Je ne m'esbaÿs de cela,
Car au pas conquester l'ala
Que tint Regnier, roy de Cecille,
Ou si bien fist et peu parla
Qu'onques Hector fist ne Troïlle.

BALLADE[122]
(pour Robert d'Estouteville)

Au poinct du jour, que l'esprevier s'esbat,
Meu de plaisir et par noble coustume,
Bruit la maulvis et de joye s'esbat,
Reçoit son per et se joinct a sa plume,
Offrir vous vueil, a ce desir m'alume,
Ioyeusement ce qu'aux amans bon semble.
Sachiez qu'Amour l'escript en son volume;
Et c'est la fin pour quoy sommes ensemble.

Dame serez de mon cuer sans debat,
Entierement, jusques mort me consume.
Lorier souef qui pour mon droit combat,
Olivier franc m'ostant toute amertume,
Raison ne veult que je desacoustume,
Et en ce vueil avec elle m'assemble,
De vous servir, mais que m'y acoustume;
Et c'est la fin pour quoy sommes ensemble.

Et qui plus est, quant dueil sur moy s'embat,
Par Fortune qui souvent si se fume,
Vostre doulx oeil sa malice rabat,
Ne plus ne moins que le vent fait la fume.
Si ne pers pas la graine que je sume
En vostre champ, quant le fruit me ressemble.
Dieu m'ordonne que le fouÿsse et fume;
Et c'est la fin pour quoy sommes ensemble.

Princesse, oyez ce que cy vous resume:
Que le mien cuer du vostre desassemble
Ja ne sera; tant de vous en presume;
Et c'est la fin pour quoy sommes ensemble.

to whom I give this ballade
for his lady, paragon of virtue.
If Love can't recompense us all like this,
I'm not surprised, for he set out
to win her at the tournament
that René held, the King of Sicily;
and there, without a word, he did as well
as ever Hector did, or Troilus.   1377

BALLADE[*]
(for Robert d'Estouteville)

At break of day, when the falcon claps his wings
from pleasure and from noble custom,
and the blackbird sings and prances in his joy,
receives his mate and joins in love with her,
within me burns desire, and I would offer you
with joy that thing which so delights all lovers.
Know that thus has Love inscribed her book,
and that is why we both are here together.   1385

You will be the lady of my heart, without debate,
entirely, until I am consumed by death.
Sweet laurel fighting by my side,
noble olive branch dispensing with all bitterness;
reason, with whom my will is to agree,
wishes I shall not become unused
to serving you, but rather grow accustomed;
and that is why we both are here together.   1393

And what is more, when grief bears down on me
through Fortune's frequent anger,
your sweet glance diminishes its malice
no more, no less, than wind blows smoke away.
I do not lose the seed I plant in your
field, when the fruit resembles me;
God wills I plow and fertilize this field,
and that is why we both are here together.   1401

Princess, listen now to what I say:
my heart will never part from yours—
this much at least I do presume,
and that is why we both are here together.   1405

CXL   Item, a sire Jehan Perdrier,
       Riens, n'a Françoys, son secont frere,[123]
       Si m'ont voulu tous jours aidier,
       Et de leurs biens faire confrere;
       Combien que Françoys, mon compere,
       Langues cuisans, flambans et rouges,
       My commandement my priere,
       Me recommanda fort a Bourges.

CXLI   Si allé veoir en Taillevent,[124]
       Ou chappitre de fricassure,
       Tout au long, derriere et devant,
       Lequel n'en parle jus ne sure.
       Mais Macquaire, je vous asseure,
       A tout let poil cuisant ung deable,
       Affin qu'il sentist bon l'arsure,
       Ce *recipe* m'escript, sans fable.

BALLADE

En realgar, en arcenic rochier,
En orpiment, en salpestre et chaulx vive,
En plomb boullant pour mieulx les esmorchier,
En suye et poix destrempez de lessive
Faicte d'estrons et de pissat de juifve,
En lavailles de jambes a meseaulx,
En racleure de piez et viels houseaulx,
En sang d'aspic et drogues venimeuses,
En fiel de loups, de regnars et blereaulx,
Soient frittes ces langues envieuses!

En cervelle de chat qui hayt peschier,
Noir, et si viel qu'il n'ait dent en gencive,
D'ung viel mastin, qui vault bien aussi chier,
Tout enragié, en sa bave et salive,
En l'escume d'une mulle poussive
Detrenchiee menu a bons ciseaulx,
En eaue ou ratz plongent groings et museaulx,
Raines, crappaulx et bestes dangereuses,
Serpens, lesars et telz nobles oyseaulx,
Soient frittes ces langues envieuses!

Item: to Sire Jean Perdrier—nothing,
nor either to François, his younger brother.
They always liked to help me
and share their goods with me,
even though François, my friend,
recommended (by both commands
and prayers) that at Bourges I try
red, flaming, searing tongues.*   1413

So I went and looked in Taillevent,
in the chapter there on fricassees;
I read it through, back and forth, up and down,
and found he didn't mention them.
But I assure you that Macquaire,
who cooked the devil within his hair
to improve the odor of his burning,
sent me this recipe.*   1421

BALLADE

In arsenic, sulphurous and pure,
in orpiment, in quicklime and saltpeter,
in boiling lead to decompose them better,
in pitch and soot soaked in lye
made up of turds and piss of Jews,
in water used to wash a leper's legs,
in things scraped from feet and old boots,
in viper's blood and poisonous drugs,
in bile of badgers, wolves and foxes,
may these envious tongues be fried!   1431

In brains of blackest cat that hates to fish
and is so old he has no teeth left in his gums,
and in the drool and drivel, which will serve as well,
of some old mastiff, mad and foaming at the mouth,
and in the lather from a wheezy mule
that's cut up fine with sharp scissors,
in water in which rats have plunged their snouts
and muzzles, along with frogs, toads and dangerous beasts,
serpents, lizards and other noble birds,
may these envious tongues be fried!   1441

En sublimé, dangereux a touchier,
Et ou nombril d'une couleuvre vive,
En sang qu'on voit es palletes sechier
Sur ces barbiers, quant plaine lune arrive,
Dont l'ung est noir, l'autre plus vert que cive,
En chancre et fiz, et en ces ors cuveaulx
Ou nourrisses essangent leurs drappeaulx,
En petiz baings de filles amoureuses
(Qui ne m'entent n'a suivy les bordeaulx)
Soient frittes ces langues envieuses!

Prince, passez tous ces frians morceaulx,
S'estamine, sacs n'avez ou bluteaulx,
Parmy le fons d'unes brayes breneuses;
Mais, par avant, en estrons de pourceaulx
Soient frittes ces langues envieuses!

CXLII Item, a maistre Andry Courault,[125]
  « Les Contrediz Franc Gontier » mande;
  Quant du tirant seant en hault,
  A cestuy la riens ne demande.
  Le Saige ne veult que contende
  Contre puissant povre homme las,
  Affin que ses fillez ne tende
  Et qu'il ne trebuche en ses las.

CXLIII Gontier ne crains: il n'a nuls hommes
  Et mieulx que moy n'est herité;
  Mais en ce debat cy nous sommes,
  Car il loue sa povreté,
  Estre povre yver et esté,
  Et a felicité repute
  Ce que tiens a maleureté.
  Lequel a tort? Or en discute.

BALLADE
(*Les contrediz de Franc Gontier*)

Sur mol duvet assis, ung gras chanoine,
Lez ung brasier, en chambre bien natee,
A son costé gisant dame Sidoine,[126]
Blanche, tendre, polie et attintee,
Boire ypocras, a jour et a nuytee,

In sublimate that's dangerous to the touch,
and in the navel of a living snake,
and in that blood one sees in barbers' rooms
drying out in bowls when full moon comes,
that's partly black, partly green as chives,
in sores and tumors, and in those filthy vats
in which wet-nurses wash their diapers,
in those little tubs that girls of pleasure use
(to understand you have to know a brothel),
may these envious tongues be fried!   1451

Prince, take all these tasty morsels,
and if you have no strainer, sieve or colander,
then pass them through the back of dirtied pants;
but before all this, in pig manure
may these envious tongues be fried!   1456

Item: to Master Andry Couraud
I send "Franc Gontier Refuted";
as for the tyrant seated up on high,
from him I ask for nothing.
The Sage has said that a man who's poor
must not contend with men of power,
lest nets be spread and he
then stumble in their meshes.*   1464

It's not Gontier I fear: he commands no men
and has no better heritage than mine;
but now we're in an argument.
He praises his own poverty
which lasts him all year long,
and he sees happiness
where I find only misery.
Who's wrong? Let's see.   1472

BALLADE
(*Franc Gontier Refuted*)

A fat canon seated on downy cushions
beside a stove in a room well-matted,
and Dame Sidoine lying at his side,
tender, white, smooth, and nicely dressed,
drinking hippocras day and night,

Rire, jouer, mignonner et baisier,
Et nu a nu, pour mieulx des corps s'aisier,
Les vy tous deux, par ung trou de mortaise:
Lors je congneus que, pour dueil appaisier,
Il n'est tresor que de vivre a son aise.

Se Franc Gontier et sa compaigne Helaine
Eussent ceste doulce vie hantee,
D'oignons, civotz, qui causent forte alaine,
N'acontassent une bise tostee.
Tout leur mathon, ne toute leur potee,
Ne prise ung ail, je le dy sans noysier.
S'ilz se vantent couchier soubz le rosier,
Lequel vault mieulx? Lict costoyé de chaise?
Qu'en dites vous? Faut il a ce musier?
Il n'est tresor que de vivre a son aise.

De gros pain bis vivent, d'orge, d'avoine,
Et boivent eaue tout au long de l'anee.
Tous les oyseaulx d'icy en Babiloine
A tel escot une seule journee
Ne me tendroient, non une matinee.
Or s'esbate, de par Dieu, Franc Gontier,
Helaine o luy, soubz le bel esglantier:
Se bien leur est, cause n'ay qu'il me poise;
Mais, quoy que soit du laboureux mestier,
Il n'est tresor que de vivre a son aise.

Prince, jugés, pour tost nous accorder.
Quant est de moy, mais qu'a nul ne desplaise,
Petit enfant, j'ay oÿ recorder:
Il n'est tresor que de vivre a son aise.

CXLIV   Item, pour ce que scet sa Bible
Ma damoiselle de Bruyeres,[127]
Donne preschier hors l'Evangille
A elle et a ses bachelieres,
Pour retraire ces villotieres
Qui ont le bec si affillé,
Mais que ce soit hors cymetieres,
Trop bien au Marchié au fillé.

laughing, playing, caressing, kissing,
and then both naked for body's greater comfort—
these two I saw by looking through a keyhole,
and then I knew that for appeasing sorrow
there is no treasure quite like living at one's ease.* 1482

If Franc Gontier and his companion Helen
had ever led a life as sweet as this,
they wouldn't give a damn for scallions
or onions which cause bad breath,
nor for their curds or stews.
(I say this without meaning harm.)
If they are proud of sleeping under rose trees,
which is better? A bed with chair nearby?
What say you? Must we waste our time on this?
There is no treasure quite like living at one's ease. 1492

They live on coarse brown bread made from oats
and barley, and all year long drink water.
All the birds from here to Babylon
could never hold me to this diet
for one day, or even for one morning.
Yet, by God, Franc Gontier has fun,
and Helen with him, beneath the wild rose tree;
if they like it, that's their business;
but whatever may be said about the Life of Work,
there is no treasure quite like living at one's ease.   1502

Prince, judge and put an end to this dispute.
But as for me (may no one take offense)
when I was young I heard it said
there is no treasure quite like living at one's ease.   1506

Item: because she knows her Bible,
My Lady de Bruyères,
I grant her and her female pupils
the right to preach from all save Gospel texts
in order to reform the girls who walk the streets
and are so sharp of tongue;
this must be done outside of graveyards
—the Linen Market would be best.*   1514

BALLADE
(*des femmes de Paris*)

Quoy qu'on tient belles langagieres
Florentines, Veniciennes,
Assez pour estre messagieres,
Et mesmement les ancïennes;
Mais, soient Lombardes, Rommaines,
Genevoises, a mes perilz,
Pimontoises, Savoisiennes,
Il n'est bon bec que de Paris.

De tres beau parler tiennent chaieres,
Se dit on, Neapolitaines,
Et sont tres bonnes caquetieres
Allemandes et Pruciennes;
Soient Grecques, Egipciennes,
De Hongrie ou d'autre pays,
Espaignolles ou Cathelennes,
Il n'est bon bec que de Paris.

Brettes, Suysses, n'y sçavent guieres,
Gasconnes, n'aussi Toulousaines:
De Petit Pont deux harengieres
Les concluront, et les Lorraines,
Engloises et Calaisiennes,
(Ay je beaucoup de lieux compris?)
Picardes de Valenciennes;
Il n'est bon bec que de Paris.

Prince, aux dames Parisiennes
De beau parler donnez le pris;
Quoy qu'on die d'Italiennes,
Il n'est bon bec que de Paris.

CXLV   Regarde m'en deux, trois, assises
Sur le bas du ply de leurs robes,
En ces moustiers, en ces eglises;
Tire toy pres, et ne te hobes;
Tu trouveras la que Macrobes[128]
Oncques ne fist tels jugemens.
Entens; quelque chose en desrobes:
Ce sont tous beaulx enseignemens.

BALLADE
(of the Women of Paris)

Even though their speech is sharp—
those girls from Florence or from Venice—
sharp enough to carry on intrigues of love
(and we'll include the ancients);
but whether it be Romans, Lombards,
Genovese (I'll stake my life on it)
or girls from Piedmont or Savoy,
there is no tongue like one from Paris.   1522

For this fine art of talking, it is said,
in Naples they appoint professors,
and the German and the Prussian women
do quite well as chatter-boxes;
but whether they be Greek, Egyptian,
or from Hungary or some other place,
or from Spain or Catalonia,
there is no tongue like one from Paris.   1530

The Bretons and the Swiss are not adept at this,
nor girls from Gascony or from Toulouse;
two fish-wives on the Petit-Pont
could shut them up, and also the Lorraines,
and those from England and Calais,
(I've named a lot of places, eh?)
and the Picard girls from Valenciennes;
there is no tongue like one from Paris.   1538

Prince, give the prize for chatter
to Parisian women; whatever
may be said about Italians,
there is no tongue like one from Paris.   1542

Look at them, in groups of twos and threes,
sitting on the hems of their long robes
in churches or in monasteries.
Get up close, but shhh! Don't move:
you'll hear pronounced such judgments
as Macrobius never dared to utter.
Listen! You'll catch some juicy morsels:
lessons such as these are worth retaining.*   1550

103

CXLVI   Item, et au mont de Montmartre,[129]
        Qui est ung lieu moult ancïen,
        Je luy donne et adjoings le tertre
        Qu'on dit le mont Valerien,
        Et, oultre plus, ung quartier d'an
        Du pardon qu'apportay de Romme:
        Si ira maint bon crestien
        En l'abbaye ou il n'entre homme.

CXLVII   Item, varletz et chamberieres
        De bons hostelz (riens ne me nuyt)
        Feront tartes, flans et goyeres,
        Et grans ralias a myenuit
        (Riens n'y font sept pintes ne huit),
        Tant que gisent seigneur et 'dame;
        Puis après, sans mener grant bruit,
        Je leur ramentoy le jeu d'asne.[130]

CXLVIII   Item, et a filles de bien,
        Qui ont peres, meres et antes,
        Par m'ame! je ne donne rien,
        Car j'ay tout donné aux servantes.
        Si fussent ilz de peu contentes:
        Grant bien leur fissent mains loppins
        Aux povres filles, entrementes
        Qui se perdent aux Jacoppins,

CXLIX   Aux Celestins et aux Chartreux;
        Quoy que vie mainent estroite,
        Si ont ilz largement entre eulx
        Dont povres filles ont souffrete;
        Tesmoing Jaqueline, et Perrete,
        Et Ysabeau qui dit: « Enné! »
        Puis qu'ilz en ont telle disette,
        A paine en seroit on damné.

CL   Item, a la Grosse Margot,[131]
        Tres doulce face et pourtraicture,
        Foy que doy *brulare bigod*,
        Assez devote creature;
        Je l'aime de propre nature,
        Et elle moy, la doulce sade:
        Qui la trouvera d'aventure,
        Qu'on luy lise ceste ballade.

Item: to the Montmartre Mount,
which is a very ancient place,
I bequeath and join the hill
that's known as Mount Valerian,
and what is more, a quarter year
from the pardon I will bring from Rome:
thus will many Christians visit this old abbey
which no man has ever entered.*   1558

Item: chambermaids and serving-men
from wealthy households (and why not?)
will make nice custards, tarts and cheesecakes
and then will whoop it up at midnight
(eight pints will barely get them going)
while lord and lady sleep;
then afterwards, as quietly as possible,
I'll give them lessons in the ass's game.*   1566

Item: those wealthy girls who still
have fathers, mothers, aunts,
upon my soul! I give them nothing,
for to their servants I have given all.
Though these poor young maids are not
demanding, some scraps could do them
lots of good—instead
they're given to the Jacobins,   1574

the Carthusians and the Celestines,
who, even though their life is strict,
usually manage to eat well
while these poor girls go hungry.
Jacqueline and Perrette will bear me witness,
and Isabelle who's always saying, "Yes, by Christ!";
but since they're always famished,
a man could hardly go to Hell for helping them. 1582

Item: Fat Margot, whose sweet face
reminds me of some painting
(upon my faith, by God)
and who is always so devout,
I love her for the way she is,
and she loves me, the dear sweet thing.
Whoever may encounter her by chance
shall read to her this ballade.*   1590

BALLADE[132]
(de la Grosse Margot)

Se j'ayme et sers la belle de bon hait,
M'en devez vous tenir ne vil ne sot?
Elle a en soy des biens a fin souhait.
Pour son amour sains bouclier et passot;
Quant viennent gens, je cours et happe ung pot,
Au vin m'en voys, sans demener grant bruit;
Je leur tens eaue, frommage, pain et fruit.
S'ilz paient bien, je leur dis: « *Bene stat*;
Retournez cy, quant vous serez en ruit,
En ce bordeau ou tenons nostre estat! »

Mais adoncques il y a grant deshait,
Quant sans argent s'en vient couchier Margot;
Veoir ne la puis, mon cuer a mort la hait.
Sa robe prens, demy saint et surcot,
Si luy jure qu'il tendra pour l'escot.
Par les costés se prent, « c'est Antecrist »
Crie, et jure par la mort Jhesucrist
Que non fera. Lors j'empoingne ung esclat;
Dessus son nez luy en fais ung escript,
En ce bordeau ou tenons nostre estat.

Puis paix se fait, et me fait ung gros pet,
Plus enflee qu'ung vlimeux escharbot.
Riant, m'assiet son poing sur mon sommet,
Gogo me dit, et me fiert le jambot.
Tous deux yvres, dormons comme ung sabot.
Et, au resveil, quant le ventre luy bruit,
Monte sur moy, que ne gaste son fruit.
Soubz elle geins, plus qu'un aiz me fait plat;
De paillarder tout elle me destruit,
En ce bordeau ou tenons nostre estat.

Vente, gresle, gelle, j'ay mon pain cuit.
Ie suis paillart, la paillarde me suit.
Lequel vault mieulx? Chascun bien s'entresuit.
L'ung vault l'autre; c'est a mau rat mau chat.
Ordure amons, ordure nous assuit;
Nous deffuyons onneur, il nous deffuit,
En ce bordeau ou tenons nostre estat.

BALLADE *
(for Fat Margot)

If I love and serve my lovely lady willingly,
should you therefore think me vile and stupid?
She has all the charms a man could want.
For love of her I gird on sword and shield;
when people come I run and grab a pot
to go get wine, as quietly as possible;
I serve them water, cheese, bread and fruit.
If they pay me well, I say, "That's good,
and please come back whenever you're in rut,
to this brothel where we ply our trade."   1600

But then bad feelings start to fly
when she comes home without a cent;
I cannot stand her, and feel a deathly hatred
for her. I grab her dress, her belt and slip,
and swear I'll make them do in place of cash.
Hands on hips, she shouts, "You Antichrist!",
and swears on Jesus' death that I
will not. So then I snatch some club
and with it write a message on her nose,
in this brothel where we ply our trade.   1610

Then we make up in bed, and she, more bloated
than a poisonous dung-hill beetle, farts
and laughs and claps me on the head,
say I'm cute and whacks my thigh.
Then, both drunk, we sleep like logs.
When we awake, her belly starts to quiver
and she mounts me, to spare love's fruit;
I groan, squashed beneath her weight—
this lechery of hers will ruin me,
in this brothel where we ply our trade.   1620

Through wind, hail or frost my living's made.
I am a lecher, and she's a lecher with me.
Which one of us is better? We're both alike:
the one as worthy as the other. Bad rat, bad cat.
We both love filth, and filth pursues us;
we flee from honor, honor flees from us,
in this brothel where we ply our trade.   1627

CLI   Item, a Marion l'Idolle[133]
Et la grant Jehanne de Bretaigne
Donne tenir publique escolle
Ou l'escollier le maistre enseigne.
Lieu n'est ou ce marchié ne tiengne,
Si non a la grisle de Mehun;
De quoy je dis: « Fy de l'enseigne,
Puis que l'ouvraige est si commun! »

CLII   Item, et a Noel Jolis,[134]
Autre chose je ne luy donne
Fors plain poing d'osiers frez cueillis
En mon jardin; je l'abandonne.
Chastoy est une belle aulmosne,
Ame n'en doit estre marry:
Unze vings coups luy en ordonne
Livrez par les mains de Henry.

CLIII   Item, ne sçay qu'a l'Ostel Dieu[135]
Donner, n'a povres hospitaulx;
Bourdes n'ont icy temps ne lieu,
Car povres gens ont assez maulx.
Chascun leur envoye leurs aulx;
Les Mendians ont eu mon oye;
Au fort, ilz en auront les os:
A menue gent menue monnoye.

CLIV   Item, je donne a mon barbier,[136]
Qui se nomme Colin Galerne,
Pres voisin d'Angelot l'erbier,
Ung gros glasson (prins ou? en Marne),
Affin qu'a son ayse s'yverne.
De l'estomac le tiengne pres;
Se l'yver ainsi se gouverne,
Il n'aura chault l'esté d'après.

CLV   Item, riens aux Enfans Trouvez;
Mais les perdus faut que consolle.
Si doivent estre retrouvez,
Par droit, sur Marion l'Idolle.
Une leçon de mon escolle
Leur lairay, qui ne dure guere.
Teste n'ayent dure ne folle;
Escoutent! car c'est la derniere.

Item: to Marion the Idol
and Big Jeanne from Britanny,
I give them leave to start a school
where pupil teaches master.
This business is transacted everywhere
(except, perhaps, the jail at Meung)
and so I say, "To Hell with signs
if this profession is so common."*   1635

Item: and to Noël Jolis
I give nothing but a bunch
of willow branches freshly picked
from my garden; and thus abandon him.
Chastisement makes good alms—
a man should not mind that.
I command two hundred twenty lashes
be given him at Henry's hands.*   1643

Item: I don't know what I'll give
the Hôtel-Dieu, or the poor hospitals;
joking would be out of place—
the poor have quite enough misfortune.
Everybody sends to them their scraps;
but the Mendicants have got my goose,
which only leaves the bones for them.
For little people, little money.*   1651

Item: I give my barber,
who's called Colin Galerne
and lives near Angelot the herbalist,
a block of ice (from where? The Marne)
to pass the winter comfortably.
He's to press it tightly to his stomach,
and if he spends the winter thus,
next summer's heat won't bother him.*   1659

Item: to the Foundlings nothing, but those
who've gone astray must be consoled:
they'll easily be found
at Marion the Idol's house.
I'll give to them a lesson
from my school—it won't last long.
Let them not be foolish or pigheaded;
listen! This lesson is the last.   1667

(Belle leçon aux enfants perdus)

CLVI
« Beaulx enfans, vous perdez la plus
Belle rose de vo chappeau;
Mes clers pres prenans comme glus,
Se vous allez a Montpipeau
Ou a Rueil, gardez la peau:
Car, pour s'esbatre en ces deux lieux,
Cuidant que vaulsist le rappeau,
Le perdit Colin de Cayeux.[137]

CLVII
« Ce n'est pas ung jeu de trois mailles,
Ou va corps, et peut estre l'ame.
Qui pert, riens n'y sont repentailles
Qu'on n'en meure a honte et diffame;
Et qui gaigne n'a pas a femme
Dido la royne de Cartage.
L'homme est donc bien fol et infame
Qui, pour si peu, couche tel gage.

CLVIII
« Qu'ung chascun encore m'escoute!
On dit, et il est verité,
Que charterie se boit toute,
Au feu l'yver, au bois l'esté:
S'argent avez, il n'est enté,
Mais le despendez tost et viste.
Qui en voyez vous herité?
Jamais mal acquest ne prouffite.

BALLADE
(de bonne doctrine)

« Car ou soies porteur de bulles,[138]
Pipeur ou hasardeur de dez,
Tailleur de faulx coings et te brusles
Comme ceulx qui sont eschaudez,
Traistres parjurs, de foy vuidez;
Soies larron, ravis ou pilles:
Ou en va l'acquest, que cuidez?
Tout aux tavernes et aux filles.

(*Advice for Children Gone Astray*)

Fair children, be careful not to lose
the finest flower in your hat;
you, my clerks, whose fingers are like glue,
if you must take to robbing
or to swindling, save your skins!
For when he tried these things
(thinking an appeal would work)
Celin de Cayeux lost his.*　　　　　　　　　　1675

It is no piddling game, this
which forfeits body, sometimes soul.
The loser, however much he may repent,
still dies in shame and infamy;
and he who wins will never marry
Dido, Queen of Carthage.
That man is base and foolish
who, for little, stakes so much.　　　　　　　1683

Now listen, everyone!
They say the profits from a cart
of wine are all consumed in winter
by the fire, in summer in the woods.
Remember, money doesn't grow on trees;
so if you have it, spend it now.
Who ever gets inheritance?
Gain ill-gotten profits no one.　　　　　　　1691

BALLADE
(*of Good Doctrine*)

Now whether you peddle indulgences,
or learn to use loaded dice,
or counterfeit coins and get burned
like those traitors without any faith
who are boiled in hot oil, or if
you're a crook who's always out filching,
where goes the money you make?
All to the girls and the taverns.*　　　　　　1699

111

« Ryme, raille, cymballe, luttes,
Comme fol, fainctif, eshontez;
Farce, broulle, joue des fleustes;
Fais, es villes et es citez,
Farces, jeux et moralitez;
Gaigne au berlanc, au glic, aux quilles:
Aussi bien va, or escoutez!
Tout aux tavernes et aux filles.

« De telz ordures te reculles?
Laboure, fauche champs et prez,
Sers et pense chevaux et mulles,
S'aucunement tu n'es lettrez;
Assez auras, se prens en grez.
Mais, se chanvre broyes ou tilles,
Ne tens ton labour qu'as ouvrez
Tout aux tavernes et aux filles?

« Chausses, pourpoins esguilletez,
Robes, et toutes vos drappilles,
Ains que vous fassiez pis, portez
Tout aux tavernes et aux filles.

CLIX   « A vous parle, compaings de galle:
Mal des ames et bien du corps,
Gardez vous tous de ce mau hasle
Qui noircist les gens quant sont mors;
Eschevez le, c'est ung mal mors;
Passez vous au mieulx que pourrez;
Et, pour Dieu, soiez tous recors
Qu'une fois viendra que mourrez. »

CLX   Item, je donne aux Quinze Vings[139]
(Qu'autant vauldroit nommer Trois Cens)
De Paris, non pas de Provins,
Car a ceulx tenu je me sens;
Ilz auront, et je m'y consens,
Sans les estuys, mes grans lunettes,
Pour mettre a part, aux Innocens,
Les gens de bien des deshonnestes.

If you rhyme, jest, play cymbals or lute
like a foolish and shameless impostor,
or if you're a mummer, magician or flutist,
or if in the towns and the cities
you do farces, plays or moralities, or if
you're a winner at dice, at cards or at ninepins,
it soon is all gone (do you hear?)
all to the girls and the taverns.   1707

Are you shocked by such evil as this?
Then go work in the fields with the farmers
and patch up the sores on horses and mules
if you don't even know how to read;
you'll be alright, if you're not too impatient.
But if you're a fellow who combs and cleans hemp,
be careful the money you make doesn't vanish
all to the girls and the taverns.   1715

Before things get worse take your pants
and your doublets of silk, your gowns
and your clothes and sell them right now
all to the girls and the taverns.   1719

To you I speak, my friends with whom I had
good times, whose souls are sick and bodies well,
be careful of the sun and wind
that turns men black when they are dead.
Stay clear of it; it's bite is evil.
Get by as best you can, and remember,
for God's sake, all of you, that the time
will come for your death too.   1727

Item: because I feel beholden
to the Fifteen Score (they might
as well be called Three Hundred)
from Paris, and not Provins,
with my consent they'll have
my glasses without their case
to tell the wicked from the good
in the graveyard of the Innocents.*   1735

CLXI   Icy n'y a ne ris ne jeu.
Que leur valut avoir chevances,
N'en grans liz de parement jeu,
Engloutir vins en grosses pances,
Mener joye, festes et dances,
Et de ce prest estre a toute heure?
Toutes faillent telles plaisances,
Et la coulpe si en demeure.

CLXII   Quant je considere ces testes
Entassees en ces charniers,
Tous furent maistres des requestes,
Au moins de la Chambre aux Deniers,[140]
Ou tous furent portepanniers:
Autant puis l'ung que l'autre dire,
Car d'evesques ou lanterniers
Je n'y congnois rien a redire.

CLXIII   Et icelles qui s'enclinoient
Unes contre autres en leurs vies,
Desquelles les unes regnoient
Des autres craintes et servies,
La les voy toutes assouvies,
Ensemble en ung tas peslemesle:
Seigneuries leur sont ravies,
Clerc ne maistre ne s'y appelle.

CLXIV   Or sont ilz mors, Dieu ait leurs ames!
Quant est des corps, ilz sont pourris,
Aient esté seigneurs ou dames,
Souef et tendrement nourris
De cresme, fromentee ou riz,
Et les oz declinent en pouldre,
Auxquelz ne chault d'esbatz ne ris.
Plaise au doulx Jhesus les absouldre!

CLXV   Aux trespassez je fais ce laiz,
Et icelluy je communique
A regens, cours, sieges, palaiz,
Hayneurs d'avarice l'inique,[141]
Lesquelz pour la chose publique
Se seichent les os et les corps:
De Dieu et de saint Dominique
Soient absols quant seront mors!

Here there is no play or laughter.
What good did it do them to have
such fortune, to lie in beds of state,
to have fat bellies filled with wine,
to hold their revels, feasts and dances,
and always to be ready for amusement?
All these pleasures vanish;
their sins alone remain.   1743

When I think of all those skulls
heaped up in charnel houses,
all once were Masters of Requests
in the Royal Treasury at least,
or perhaps just simple porters;
I do not know which one is which;
I can no longer tell you
who was a bishop or a lantern-maker.*   1751

And those women who once bowed
and scraped to one another,
and some of whom commanded
while the others served in fear,
I see them now dead and gone,
their bodies heaped in piles,
their lands usurped; for clerk
or master there is no appeal.   1759

Now they're dead, God rest their souls!
As for their bodies, they've all rotted,
they who once were lords and ladies
and lived on sweet, tender foods
like puddings, creams and rice,
and their bones now turn to powder
and have little thought of joy or laughter.
May Sweet Jesus absolve them all.   1767

For those dead and gone I write
this legacy, and make it known to regents,
courts, tribunals and seats of justice,
who all hate the crime of avarice,
and who, for public weal,
dry out their bones and bodies.
May God and Saint Dominic
absolve them when they die.*   1775

115

CLXVI   Item, riens a Jacquet Cardon,[142]
Car je n'ay riens pour luy d'honneste,
Non pas que le gette habandon,
Sinon ceste bergeronnette;
S'elle eust le chant « Marionnette »,
Fait pour Marion la Peautarde,
Ou d' « Ouvrez vostre huys, Guillemette »,
Elle allast bien a la moustarde:

CHANSON

Au retour de dure prison,[143]
Ou j'ai laissié presque la vie,
Se Fortune a sur moy envie,
Jugiez s'elle fait mesprison!
Il me semble que, par raison,
Elle deust bien estre assouvie
       Au retour.

Se si plaine est de desraison
Que vueille que du tout devie,
Plaise a Dieu que l'ame ravie
En soit lassus en sa maison,
       Au retour!

CLXVII   Item, donne a maistre Lomer,[144]
Comme extraict que je suis de fee,
Qu'il soit bien amé (mais d'amer
Fille en chief ou femme coeffee,
Ja n'en ayt la test eschauffee)
Et qu'il ne luy couste une noix
Faire ung soir cent fois la faffee,
En despit d'Ogier le Danois.

CLXVIII   Item, donne aux amans enfermes,
Sans le laiz maistre Alain Chartier,[145]
A leurs chevez, de pleurs et lermes
Trestout fin plain ung benoistier,
Et ung petit brain d'esglantier,
En tous temps vert, pour guipillon,
Pourveu qu'ilz diront ung psaultier
Pour l'ame du povre Villon.

Item: to Jacquet Cardon—nothing,
since I have nothing decent for him
(mind you, I won't abandon him),
except perhaps this little song.
If it could have the tune of "Marionette"
composed for Marion la Peautarde,
or that of "Open up your door, Guillemette,"
it might then serve for getting mustard.*   1783

SONG

On my return from that harsh prison
in which I almost gave my life,
if Fate still has designs on me,
you judge if she be wrong.
It would seem that by all reason
she should now be satisfied,
    on my return.*   1790

If she is so unjust that she
would wish I pass away and die,
please God that He may take
my soul to His abode on high,
    on my return.   1795

Item: I bequeath to Master Lomer,
since I was born of fairies,
the gift of being well-loved (but let
him not get heated up with love
for girls who go bareheaded or wear hats),
and let it cost him not a cent
to make love a hundred times a night,
in spite of great Ogier the Dane.*   1803

Item: I bequeath to pining lovers,
besides Alain Chartier's fine legacy,
a holy-water basin filled with tears
to put beside their bed,
and a little sprig of wild rose,
forever green, to sprinkle with,
provided they recite some psalms
for the soul of poor Villon.*   1811

117

CLXIX   Item, a maistre Jacques James,[146]
Qui se tue d'amasser biens,
Donne fiancer tant de femmes
Qu'il vouldra; mais d'espouser? riens.
Pour qui amasse il? Pour les siens?
Il ne plaint fors que ses morceaulx:
Ce qui fut aux truyes, je tiens
Qu'il doit de droit estre aux pourceaulx.

CLXX   Item, le camus Seneschal,[147]
Qui unes foys paia mes debtes,
En recompence, mareschal
Sera, pour ferrer oyes, canettes.
Je luy envoie ces sornettes
Pour soy desennuyer; combien,
S'il veult, face en des alumettes:
De bien chanter s'ennuye on bien.

CLXXI   Item, au Chevalier du Guet[148]
Je donne deux beaulx petiz pages,
Philebert et le gros Marquet,
Lesquelz servy, dont sont plus sages,
La plus partie de leurs aages,
Ont le provost des mareschaulx.
Helas! s'ilz sont cassez de gages,
Aller les fauldra tous deschaulx.

CLXXII   Item, a Chappelain[149] je laisse
Ma chappelle a simple tonsure,
Chargiee d'une seiche messe
Ou il ne fault pas grant lecture.
Resigné luy eusse ma cure,
Mais point ne veult de charge d'ames;
De confesser, ce dit, n'a cure,
Sinon chamberieres et dames.

CLXXIII   Pour ce que scet bien mon entente
Jehan de Calais,[150] honnorable homme,
Qui ne me vit des ans a trente
Et ne scet comment je me nomme,
De tout ce testament, en somme,
S'aucun' y a difficulté,
L'oster jusqu'au rez d'une pomme
Je luy en donne faculté.

Item: to Master Jacques James,
who kills himself amassing wealth,
I grant he be betrothed to all the girls
he wants; but then to marry? None.
He hoards for whom? For his own family?
His only grief is for the food he eats.
The filth of sows, I think,
by right belongs to hogs.*   1819

Item: the snub-nosed Seneschal,
who once paid off my debts
in recompense will be
a blacksmith shoeing geese and ducks.
I send along these jokes in hopes
they will amuse him; but if he wants,
I'll let him roll them up to use as matches:
good singing, too, gets boring.*   1827

Item: to the Captain of the Watch
I give two handsome page-boys,
Philibert and fat Marquet,
who, throughout their lives
(and now are wiser for it),
have served the Provost Marshal.
Alas! but if they now are fired,
they'll have to both go barefoot.*   1835

Item: to Chappelain I leave
my humble clerk's chapel;
he will not have to do much reading
to recite its one dry mass.
I'd also give to him my vicarship,
but I don't think he wants the care of souls;
he says he doesn't like confessions, excepting
those of chambermaids and ladies.*   1843

Because he understands my meaning,
to Jean de Calais, a man of honor,
who hasn't seen me all these thirty years
and doesn't know my name, if he finds
there are some difficulties in this
testament, I hereby give permission
for him to prune it
like an apple tree.*   1851

119

CLXXIV De le gloser et commenter,
De le diffinir et descripre,
Diminuer ou augmenter,
De le canceller et prescripre
De sa main et ne sceut escripre,
Interpreter et donner sens,
A son plaisir, meilleur ou pire:
A tout cecy je m'y consens.

CLXXV Et s'aucun, dont n'ay congnoissance,
Estoit allé de mort a vie,[151]
Je vueil et luy donne puissance,
Affin que l'ordre soit suyvie,
Pour estre mieulx parassouvie,
Que ceste aumosne ailleurs transporte,
Sans se l'appliquer par envie:
A son ame je m'en rapporte.

CLXXVI Item, j'ordonne a Sainte Avoye,[152]
Et non ailleurs, ma sepulture;
Et, afin q'un chascun me voie,
Non pas en char, mais en painture,
Que l'on tire mon estature
D'ancre, s'il ne coustoit trop chier.
De tombel? riens: je n'en ay cure,
Car il greveroit le planchier.

CLXXVII Item, vueil qu'autour de ma fosse
Ce qui s'ensuit, sans autre histoire,
Soit escript en lettre assez grosse,
Et qui n'auroit point d'escriptoire,
De charbon ou de pierre noire,
Sans en riens entamer le plastre;
Au moins sera de moi memoire,
Telle qu'elle est d'ung bon follastre:

EPITAPHE

CLXXVIII CY GIST ET DORT EN CE SOLLIER,
QU'AMOURS OCCIST DE SON RAILLON,
UNG POVRE PETIT ESCOLLIER,
QUI FUT NOMMÉ FRANÇOYS VILLON.
ONCQUES DE TERRE N'EUT SILLON.
IL DONNA TOUT, CHASCUN LE SCET:
TABLES, TRESTEAULX, PAIN, CORBEILLON.
GALLANS, DICTES EN CE VERSET:

To gloss, annotate,
define, transcribe,
diminish or augment,
cancel and suppress
with his own hand, and if
he cannot write, to interpret
at his pleasure, for better or for worse;
to all this I herewith consent.   1859

And if someone has passed from
death to life without my knowing it,
I wish and do empower said
Calais to carry out my plan
and see that it's fulfilled,
and that these alms be given others
without his keeping them through greed:
I leave it to his conscience.*   1867

Item: I command that I be buried
at Sainte Avoye, not elsewhere;
and so that everyone can see me
(not in the flesh, but in a picture)
let a full-length portrait be done of me
in ink, if it won't cost too much.
A tomb? No, it doesn't matter; besides
it just might overload the floor.*   1875

Item: I will that about my grave,
what follows, without adornment,
be written in large letters,
and if there is no ink around,
with carbon or black stone,
carefully, so as not to break the plaster.
And thus I'll be remembered as a man
who liked to have good times.   1883

EPITAPH

HERE LIES IN SLUMBER IN THIS UPSTAIRS ROOM
A MAN KILLED BY LOVE'S ARROWS,
A POOR WORTHLESS SCHOLAR
WHO WAS CALLED FRANÇOIS VILLON:
HE NEVER OWNED A FURROW IN A FIELD.
HE GAVE ALL AWAY, AS IS WELL KNOWN,
TABLES, BEDS, BREAD AND BASKET.
GALLANTS, RECITE FOR HIM THIS VERSE: 1891

VERSET
(*ou rondeau*)

REPOS ETERNEL DONNE A CIL,[153]
SIRE, ET CLARTÉ PERPETUELLE,
QUI VAILLANT PLAT NE ESCUELLE
N'EUT ONCQUES, N'UNG BRAIN DE PERCIL.
IL FUT REZ, CHIEF, BARBE ET SOURCIL,
COMME UNG NAVET QU'ON RET OU PELLE.
REPOS ETERNEL DONNE A CIL.

RIGUEUR LE TRANSMIT EN EXIL
ET LUY FRAPPA AU CUL LA PELLE,
NON OBSTANT QU'IL DIT: « J'EN APPELLE! »
QUI N'EST PAS TERME TROP SUBTIL.
REPOS ETERNEL DONNE A CIL.

CLXXIX   Item, je vueil qu'on sonne a bransle
Le gros beffroy, qui est de voirre;[154]
Combien qu'il n'est cuer qui ne tremble,
Quant de sonner est a son erre.
Sauvé a mainte belle terre;
Le temps passé, chascun le scet:
Fussent gens d'armes ou tonnerre,
Au son de luy, tout mal cessoit.

CLXXX   Les sonneurs auront quatre miches
Et, se c'est peu, demye douzaine;
Autant n'en donnent les plus riches,
Mais ilz seront de saint Estienne.[155]
Vollant est homme de grant paine:
L'ung en sera; quant g'y regarde,
Il en vivra une sepmaine.
Et l'autre? Au fort, Jehan de la Garde.

CLXXXI   Pour tout ce fournir et parfaire,
J'ordonne mes executeurs,
Auxquels fait bon avoir affaire
Et contentent bien leurs debteurs.
Ilz ne sont pas moult grans vanteurs
Et ont bien de quoy, Dieu mercis!
De ce fait seront directeurs.
Escry: je t'en nommerai six.

VERSE
(*or Rondeau*)

GRANT HIM ETERNAL REST,
O LORD, AND EVERLASTING LIGHT
TO HIM WHO NEVER OWNED A PLATE
OR BOWL OR SPRIG OF PARSLEY.
HIS EYEBROWS, BEARD AND HEAD WERE SHAVED
AS ONE MIGHT SHAVE OR PEEL A TURNIP.
GRANT HIM ETERNAL REST.*   1898

HARSH JUSTICE BANISHED HIM
AND WHACKED HIM WITH A SHOVEL ON HIS ARSE,
ALTHOUGH HE SHOUTED "I APPEAL!",
A PHRASE THAT'S NOT TOO SUBTLE.
GRANT HIM ETERNAL REST.   1903

Item: I command they peal the great bell,
the one that's made of glass,
although there is no heart
that does not tremble when it rings.
Many fine lands it's saved
in times past, as all men know.
Whether it be men-at-arms or thunder,
at its sound all evil stops.*   1911

The ringers shall receive four loaves,
and if that's too little, half a dozen
(the richest men don't give *that* much),
but they will be Saint Stephen's kind.
Volant's a careful man: he'll be
one of them; but when I think of it,
I know his share will last him one whole week.
The other? Why not Jean de la Garde?*   1919

To accomplish and achieve all this,
I now name my executors,
such men as like to do this work
and keep their debtors happy, too.
They're not great braggarts,
yet rich enough, thank God!
I'm sure they'll see this through.
Now write! I'll name you six.   1927

CLXXXII   C'est maistre Martin Bellefaye,[156]
Lieutenant du cas criminel.
Qui sera l'autre? G'y pensoye:
Ce sera sire Colombel;
S'il luy plaist et il luy est bel,
Il entreprendra ceste charge.
Et l'autre? Michiel Jouvenel.
Ces trois seulz, et pour tout, j'en charge.

CLXXXIII   Mais, ou cas qu'ilz s'en excusassent,
En redoubtant les premiers frais,
Ou totallement recusassent,
Ceulx qui s'enssuivent cy après
Institue, gens de bien tres:
Phelip Brunel, noble escuyer,[157]
Et l'autre, son voisin d'emprès,
Si est maistre Jaques Raguier,

CLXXXIV   Et l'autre, maistre Jaques James,
Trois hommes de bien et d'onneur,
Desirans de sauver leurs ames
Et doubtans Dieu Nostre Seigneur.
Plus tost y mecteront du leur
Que ceste ordonnance ne baillent;
Point n'auront de contrerolleur,
Mais a leur bon plaisir en taillent.

CLXXXV   Des testamens qu'on dit le Maistre
De mon fait n'aura *quid* ne *quod*;
Mais ce sera ung jeune prestre,
Qui est nommé Thomas Tricot.[158]
Voulentiers beusse a son escot,
Et qu'il me coustast ma cornete!
S'il sceust jouer a ung tripot,
Il eust de moy *le Trou Perrete*.

CLXXXVI   Quant au regart du luminaire,
Guillaume du Ru[159] j'y commetz.
Pour porter les coings du suaire,
Aux executeurs le remetz.
Trop plus mal me font qu'onques mais
Barbe, cheveulx, penil, sourcis.
Mal me presse, temps desormais
Que crie a toutes gens mercis.

First there's Master Marin
Bellefaye, Criminal Lieutenant.
Who'll be next? I thought
it might be Sire Colombel;
if he thinks it might be pleasant
and convenient, he'll have this job.
And next? Michel Jouvenel.
These three alone will be in charge.*   1935

But in the event they excuse themselves
from fear of initial costs,
or entirely refuse the job,
those hereinafter named
I institute, fine men all three:
Philippe Brunel, a noble squire,
and next, his closest neighbor,
Master Jacques Raguier,*   1943

and lastly, Master Jacques James:
three good, honorable men
seeking their souls' salvation
and fearing the Lord our God.
They're men who'd rather give their own
than not fulfil this ordinance.
They'll have no one controlling them;
they'll do exactly as they wish.   1951

The Probate Court
won't get a thing from me,
but rather a young priest
who's called Thomas Tricot.
I'd gladly have a drink on him,
although it might cost me my hat!
If he knew how to play court tennis,
I'd give him *Perrette's Hole.**   1959

As for the funeral lamps,
Guillaume du Ru will be in charge;
as to who will bear the pall,
I leave that task to my executors.
Now more than ever my beard, hair,
groin and eyebrows cause me pain.
I'm pressed with ills. It's time
I cried to one and all for pardon.*   1967

125

BALLADE
(*de mercy*)

A Chartreux et a Celestins,[160]
A Mendians et a Devotes,
A musars et claquepatins,
A servans et filles mignotes
Portans surcotz et justes cotes,
A cuidereaux d'amours transsis
Chaussans sans meshaing fauves botes,
Je crie a toutes gens mercis.

A filletes monstrans tetins
Pour avoir plus largement hostes,
A ribleurs, mouveurs de hutins,
A bateleurs, traynans marmotes,
A folz, folles, a sotz et sotes,
Qui s'en vont siflant six a six,
A marmosetz et mariotes,
Je crie a toutes gens mercis.

Sinon aux traistres chiens matins,[161]
Qui m'ont fait chier dures crostes
Maschier mains soirs et mains matins,
Qu'ores je ne crains pas trois crotes.
Je feisse pour eulx petz et rotes;
Je ne puis, car je suis assis.
Au fort, pour eviter riotes,
Je crie a toutes gens mercis.

Qu'on leur froisse les quinze costes
De gros mailletz, fors et massis,
De plombees et telz pelotes.
Je crie a toutes gens mercis.

BALLADE
(of Pardon)

To Carthusians, Celestines,
to Mendicants, *Filles-Dieu*,
to loafers, dandies, servants
and courtesans who wear
surcoats and skin-tight robes,
to lovesick fops who wear
tan boots without complaining,
to one and all I cry for pardon.*   1975

To whores who let their breasts
be seen to catch more clients,
to swindlers, brawlers,
to showmen with trained apes,
to fools and those who play
in farces, whistling six abreast,
to little boys and girls,
to one and all I cry for pardon.   1983

Except to those vile sons of bitches
who made me gnaw hard crusts
of bread so many nights and mornings
that I no longer give a damn.
I'd make them gifts of farts and belches,
except I can't—I'm sitting down.
But anyhow, to avoid more fights,
to one and all I cry for pardon.*   1991

Let their ribs be mauled
with good stout mallets,
with cudgels and balls of lead.
To one and all I cry for pardon.   1995

AUTRE BALLADE

Icy se clost le testament
Et finist du pauvre Villon.
Venez a son enterrement,
Quant vous orrez le carrillon,
Vestus rouge com vermillon,[162]
Car en amours mourut martir:
Ce jura il sur son couillon,
Quant de ce monde voult partir.

Et je croy bien que pas n'en ment;
Car chassié fut comme ung souillon
De ses amours hayneusement,
Tant que, d'icy a Roussillon,
Brosse n'y a ne brossillon
Qui n'eust, ce dit il sans mentir,
Ung lambeau de son cotillon,
Quant de ce monde voult partir.

Il est ainsi et tellement,
Quant mourut n'avoit qu'ung haillon;
Qui plus, en mourant, mallement
L'espoignoit d'Amours l'esguillon;
Plus agu que le ranguillon
D'ung baudrier luy faisoit sentir
(C'est de quoy nous esmerveillon),
Quant de ce monde voult partir.

Prince, gent comme esmerillon,
Sachiez qu'il fist au departir:
Ung traict but de vin morillon,
Quant de ce monde voult partir.

OTHER BALLADE

Here ends and finishes
the Testament of Poor Villon.
When next you hear the passing-bell,
come ye to his burial
all dressed in brightest red,
for he died Love's martyr:
this he swore upon one testicle
when he prepared to leave this world.*   2003

I'm sure that he's not lying; his love
chased him away as if he were
some filthy wretch, so spitefully
that all the way from here to Roussillon
there is no bush or shrub
which did not have (this is the truth)
some tatters from his shirt,
when he prepared to leave this world.   2011

Thus and so it is, that when he died
he only owned a single rag;
what's more, while he was dying
Love foully stabbed him with his dart
and caused him pain more piercing
than from a buckle-tongue
(which caused us much astonishment),
when he prepared to leave this world.   2019

Prince, as gently bred as a falcon,
hear now what he did on his departure:
he took a gulp of dark red wine
when he prepared to leave this world.   2023

Poésies Diverses / *Miscellaneous Poems*

POÉSIES DIVERSES

I — BALLADE[163]
(de bon conseil)

Hommes faillis, bersaudez de raison,
Desnaturez et hors de congnoissance,
Desmis du sens, comblez de desraison,
Fols abusez, plains de descongnoissance,
Qui procurez contre vostre naissance,
Vous soubzmettans a detestable mort
Par lascheté, las! que ne vous remort
L'orribleté qui a honte vous maine?
Voyez comment maint jeunes homs est mort
Par offenser et prendre autruy demaine.

Chascun en soy voye sa mesprison,
Ne nous venjons, prenons en pacience;
Nous congnoissons que ce monde est prison
Aux vertueux franchis d'impatience;
Battre, rouiller, pour ce n'est pas science,
Tollir, ravir, piller, meurtrir a tort.
De Dieu ne chault, trop de verté se tort
Qui en telz faiz sa jeunesse demaine,
Dont a la fin ses poins doloreux tort
Par offenser et prendre autruy demaine.

Que vault piper, flater, rire en trayson,
Quester,[164] mentir, affermer sans fiance,
Farcer, tromper, artifier poison,
Vivre en pechié, dormir en deffiance
De son prouchain sans avoir confiance?
Pour ce conclus: de bien faisons effort,
Reprenons cuer, ayons en Dieu confort,
Nous n'avons jour certain en la sepmaine;
De nos maulx ont noz parens le ressort
Par offenser et prendre autruy demaine.

MISCELLANEOUS POEMS

I — BALLADE*
(of Good Counsel)

O soul-sick men, barred from reason,
perverted, beyond consciousness,
deranged, no longer rational,
deluded fools filled with ignorance,
who seek to soil your birthright
submitting yourselves thus to hateful death
through weakness, alas! Does not the horror
of your shame make you remorseful?
Think how many youths have died
through vice and taking others' property.   10

Each man can see his own mistakes;
we must be unrevengeful, patient.
We know this world to be a prison, even
for the blessed freed from all impatience;
and so to fight, battle, steal, ravish,
pillage or kill in sin are errors.
He who leads a youth like this cares not
for God, and wanders from the paths of truth;
and in the end he wrings his hands in grief
through vice and taking others' property.   20

What is it worth to cheat and flatter, laugh
in treachery, to take collections, to lie, swear
dishonestly, deceive, betray, make poison,
live in sin, and sleep mistrusting
neighbors, lacking faith in them?
So I conclude: we must make efforts to be good,
take heart, and in Our Lord find comfort;
we never can be sure of days to come.
Our sins reflect upon our parents,
through vice and taking others' property.*   30

133

Vivons en paix, exterminons discort;
Ieunes et vieulx, soyons tous d'ung accort:
La loy le veult, l'apostre le ramaine
Licitement en l'epistre rommaine;
Ordre nous fault, estat ou aucun port.
Notons ces poins; ne laissons le vray port
Par offenser et prendre autruy demaine.

II – BALLADE
(des proverbes)

Tant grate chievre que mal gist,
Tant va le pot a l'eaue qu'il brise,
Tant chauffe on le fer qu'il rougist,
Tant le maille on qu'il se debrise,
Tant vault l'homme comme on le prise,
Tant s'eslongne il qu'il n'en souvient,
Tant mauvais est qu'on le desprise,
Tant crie l'on Noel qu'il vient.

Tant parle on qu'on se contredist,
Tant vault bon bruyt que grace acquise,
Tant promet on qu'on s'en desdist,
Tant prie on que chose est acquise,
Tant plus est chiere et plus est quise,
Tant la quiert on qu'on y parvient,
Tant plus commune et moins requise,
Tant crie l'on Noel qu'il vient.

Tant ayme on chien qu'on le nourrist,
Tant court chanson qu'elle est apprise,
Tant garde on fruit qu'il se pourrist,
Tant bat on place qu'elle est prise,
Tant tarde on que faut entreprise,
Tant se haste on que mal advient,
Tant embrasse on que chiet la prise,
Tant crie l'on Noel qu'il vient.

Tant raille on que plus on n'en rit,
Tant despent on qu'on n'a chemise,
Tant est on franc que tout y frit,
Tant vault « tien » que chose promise,

Let us live in peace, abolish dissidence,
let old and young be yet of one accord:
the law demands, the Apostle justly tells us
in his Epistle to the Romans.
We must have order, station or some fixed place.
Let us take note and not forsake our destiny
through vice and taking others' property.   37

II – BALLADE
(of Proverbs)

So much a goat scratches that he spoils his bed,
so much goes the pitcher to the well that it breaks,
so much is the iron heated that it reddens,
so much is it hammered that it cracks,
so much are men worth as other men see them,
so much a man journeys that he is forgotten,
so much is he bad that he is despised,
so much does one cry out Noël that it comes.   8

so much does one talk that one ends by refuting oneself,
so much is fame worth that it brings men's good graces,
so much does one promise that one has to back down,
so much does one pray that one's wish is fulfilled,
so much is it dear, the more it is wanted,
so much is it wanted that one finally obtains it,
so much is it common, the less it is needed,
so much does one cry out Noël that it comes.   16

So much are dogs loved that they're fed,
so much are songs heard that they're learnt,
so much is fruit kept that it spoils,
so much is a city besieged that it falls,
so much does one linger that one loses the chance,
so much does one hasten that things are done badly,
so much does one try that all is then lost,
so much does one cry out Noël that it comes.   24

So much does one rant that one ceases to laugh,
so much does one spend that one loses one's shirt,
so much is one kind that one spends all there is,
so much are worth gifts as things that are promised,

Tant ayme on Dieu qu'on suit l'Eglise,
Tant donne on qu'emprunter convient,
Tant tourne vent qu'il chiet en bise,
Tant crie l'on Noel qu'il vient.

Prince, tant vit fol qu'il s'avise,
Tant va il qu'après il revient,
Tant le mate on qu'il se ravise,
Tant crie l'on Noel qu'il vient.

III — BALLADE
(*des menus propos*)

Je congnois bien mouches en let,[165]
Je congnois a la robe l'homme,
Je congnois le beau temps du let,
Je congnois au pommier la pomme,
Je congnois l'arbre a veoir la gomme,
Je congnois quant tout est de mesmes,
Je congnois qui besongne ou chomme,
Je congnois tout, fors que moy mesmes.

Je congnois pourpoint au colet,
Je congnois le moyne a la gonne,
Je congnois le maistre au varlet.
Je congnois au voille la nonne,
Je congnois quant pipeur jargonne,
Je congnois fols nourris de cresmes,
Je congnois le vin a la tonne,
Je congnois tout, fors que moy mesmes.

Je congnois cheval et mulet,
Je congnois leur charge et leur somme,
Je congnois Bietris et Belet,
Je congnois get qui nombre et somme,
Je congnois vision et somme,
Je congnois la faulte des Boesmes,[166]
Je congnois le povoir de Romme,
Je congnois tout, fors que moy mesmes.

Prince, je congnois tout en somme,
Je congnois coulourez et blesmes,
Je congnois Mort qui tout consomme,
Je congnois tout, fors que moy mesmes.

so much one loves God that one goes off to church,
so much does one give that it's better to lend,
so much the wind turns that it blows icy cold,
so much does one cry out Noël that it comes.   32

Prince, so much a fool lives that he's cured,
so much does he wander that he later returns,
so much is he humbled that he changes his mind,
so much does one cry out Noël that it comes.   36

III – BALLADE
(of Small Talk)

I know flies in the milk,
I know men by their clothes,
I know good from bad weather,
I know fruit by its color,
I know trees by their sap,
I know when all is the same,
I know who's busy or idle,
I know all, save myself.*   8

I know doublets by their collars,
I know monks by their robes,
I know masters by their servants,
I know nuns by their veils,
I know con-men by their slang,
I know fools fed on cheese,
I know wine by its cask,
I know all, save myself.   16

I know horses and mules,
I know the load they can carry,
I know Marys and Janes,
I know counting and adding,
I know visions and sleep,
I know heresies of Hussites,
I know the power of Rome,
I know all, save myself.*   24

Prince, I know all, in short,
I know pink cheeks from wan,
I know Death all-devouring,
I know all, save myself.   28

IV – BALLADE
(*des contre vérités*)

Il n'est soing que quant on a fain,
Ne service que d'ennemy,
Ne maschier qu'ung botel de foing,
Ne fort guet que d'homme endormy,
Ne clemence que felonnie,
N'asseurence que de peureux,
Ne foy que d'homme qui regnie,
Ne bien conseillé qu'amoureux.

Il n'est engendrement qu'en boing,
Ne bon bruit que d'homme banny,
Ne ris qu'après ung coup de poing,
Ne lotz que debtes mettre en ny,
Ne vraye amour qu'en flaterie,
N'encontre que de maleureux,
Ne vray rapport que menterie,
Ne bien conseillé qu'amoureux.

Ne tel repos que vivre en soing,
N'honneur porter que dire: « Fi! »,
Ne soy vanter que de faulx coing,
Ne santé que d'homme bouffy,
Ne hault vouloir que couardie,
Ne conseil que de furieux,
Ne doulceur qu'en femme estourdie,
Ne bien conseillé qu'amoureux.

Voulez vous que verté vous die?
Il n'est jouer qu'en maladie,
Lettre vraye que tragedie,
Lasche homme que chevalereux,
Orrible son que melodie,
Ne bien conseillé qu'amoureux.

IV — BALLADE
(of Counter-Truths)

There is no care save when one's hungry,
nor service save from enemy,
nor teeth except in pile of hay,
nor guard like that of a man asleep,
nor clemency except in felony,
nor surety except from fearful man,
nor faith except from an apostate,
nor wisdom save from those in love.   8

There's no begetting save in baths,
nor fame except from exiled man,
nor laughter save from blow of fist,
nor praise except from debts denied,
nor constant love except in flattery,
nor meeting save of men in misery,
nor understanding save through lies,
nor wisdom save from those in love,   16

nor rest like that of worried life,
nor honor save in saying, "Hell!",
nor pride except in counterfeiting,
nor health except in men all bloated,
nor act of will except in cowardice,
nor counsel save from man enraged,
nor sweetness save from hare-brained woman,
nor wisdom save from those in love.   24

You want the truth from me?
There is no joy except in sickness,
nor truth outside the theater,
nor coward like a knightly man,
nor grimmer sound than melody,
nor wisdom save from those in love.   30

V – BALLADE[167]

(*contre les ennemis de la France*)

Rancontré soit des bestes feu gectans,
Que Jason vit, querant la toison d'or;
Ou transmué d'homme en beste sept ans,
Ainsi que fut Nabugodonosor;
Ou perte il ait et guerre aussi villaine
Que les Troyens pour la prinse d'Helaine;
Ou avallé soit avec Tantalus
Et Proserpine aux infernaulx palus;
Ou plus que Job soit en griefve souffrance,
Tenant prison en la tour Dedalus,
Qui mal vouldroit au royaulme de France!

Quatre mois soit en ung vivier chantans,
Le teste au fons, ainsi que le butor;
Ou au Grant Turc vendu deniers contans,
Pour estre mis au harnois comme ung tor;
Ou trente ans soit, comme la Magdalaine,
Sans drap vestir de linge ne de laine;
Ou soit noyé comme fut Narcisus,
Ou aux cheveulx, comme Absalon, pendus
Ou, comme fut Judas, par Desperance;
Ou puist perir comme Simon Magus,
Qui mal vouldroit au royaulme de France!

D'Octovien puist revenir le tems:
C'est qu'on luy coule au ventre son tresor;
Ou qu'il soit mis entre meules flotans
En ung moulin, comme fut saint Victor;
Ou transglouty en la mer, sans aleine,
Pis que Jonas ou corps de la baleine;
Ou soit banny de la clarté Phebus,
Des biens Juno et du soulas Venus,
Et du dieu Mars soit pugny a oultrance,
Ainsy que fut roy Sardanapalus,
Qui mal vouldroit au royaulme de France!

Prince, porté soit des serfs Eolus
En la forest ou domine Glaucus;
Ou privé soit de paix et d'esperance:
Car digne n'est de posseder vertus
Qui mal vouldroit au royaulme de France!

V — BALLADE*
(*against the Enemies of France*)

May he encounter those monsters belching fire
which Jason saw while seeking the Golden Fleece,
or yet be changed from man to beast for seven
years, as once was Nebuchadnezzar,
or may he suffer loss and war as horrible
as that of Trojans for the rape of Helen;
or may he be thrown down with Tantalus
and Proserpine into infernal marshes;
or more than Job may he have grievous suffering,
and prison in the Labyrinth of Dedalus,
he who wishes evil on the realm of France.   11

Or may he pass four months head downwards
in some fishpond, howling like a bittern;
or to the Grand Turk be sold for cash
and then be put in harness like a bull;
or may he go, like Magdalen, for thirty years
without a stitch of clothes, of linen or of wool;
or drown himself as did Narcissus,
or by his hair, like Absalom, be hung,
or yet like Judas, through despair;
or may he perish as did Simon Magus,
he who wishes evil on the realm of France.   22

May Octavian's time return in order that
his molten treasure be poured into his belly;
may he be placed between two moving grindstones
in a windmill like Saint Victor;
or, breathless, be swallowed up into the ocean
worse than Jonah in the body of the whale;
or yet be banished from Phoebus' light,
Juno's wealth, or from the joys of Venus,
or be punished to the death by Mars
as was Sardanapalus, the King,
he who wishes evil on the realm of France.   33

Prince, let him be carried by Aeolus' servants
into the sea where Glaucus rules;
or be deprived of peace and hope
through being unworthy of possessing virtue,
he who wishes evil on the realm of France.   38

VI – RONDEAU[168]

Jenin l'Avenu,
Va-t-en aux estuves;
Et toy la venu,
Jenin l'Avenu,

Si te lave nud
Et te baigne es cuvcs.
Jenin l'Avenu,
Va-t-en aux estuves.

VII – BALLADE[169]

(*du concours de Blois*)

Je meurs de seuf après de la fontaine,
Chault comme feu, et tremble dent a dent;
En mon païs suis en terre loingtaine;
Lez ung brasier frissonne tout ardent;
Nu comme ung ver, vestu en president,
Je ris en pleurs et attens sans espoir;
Confort reprens en triste desespoir;
Je m'esjouÿs et n'ay plaisir aucun;
Puissant je suis sans force et sans povoir,
Bien recueully, debouté de chascun.

Rien ne m'est seur que la chose incertaine;
Obscur, fors ce qui est tout evident;
Doubte ne fais, fors en chose certaine;
Science tiens a soudain accident;
Je gaigne tout et demeure perdent;
Au point du jour dis: « Dieu vous doint bon soir! »
Gisant envers, j'ay grant paour de cheoir;
J'ay bien de quoy et si n'en ay pas ung;
Eschoitte attens et d'omme ne suis hoir,
Bien recueully, debouté de chascun.

De riens n'ay soing, si mectz toute ma paine
D'acquerir biens et n'y suis pretendent;
Qui mieulx me dit, c'est cil qui plus m'attaine,
Et qui plus vray, lors plus me va bourdent;
Mon amy est, qui me fait entendent

142

VI — RONDEAU*

Jenin l'Avenu,
go take a bath;
and when you're there,
Jenin l'Avenu,

take off your clothes
and use the tub.
Jenin l'Avenu,
go take a bath.

VII — BALLADE*
(*for the Contest at Blois*)

I die of thirst beside the fountain,
as hot as fire, trembling tooth on tooth;
in my own country I'm in a far-off land;
beside a fire I shiver, all aflame;
as naked as a worm, yet richly dressed in furs;
I laugh through tears, and wait without a hope;
my only comfort is in sad despair;
I rejoice and have no pleasure;
I am strong, but have no force or power,
well received, rebuffed by all.   10

Nothing's sure save what is yet uncertain,
nor more obscure than what is evident;
I have no doubts save when I'm positive;
in sudden accident is knowledge based;
I win all and yet remain the loser;
at break of day I say, "Goodnight";
when I lie down I have great fear of falling;
I'm quite well off and yet don't have a penny;
I await inheritance and yet am no man's heir,
well received, rebuffed by all.   20

I'm never careful, but I make all efforts
to acquire wealth though I have none to claim;
who to me is nicest most annoys me;
who speaks the truth tells me most lies;
my friend is he who leads me to believe

143

D'ung cigne blanc que c'est ung corbeau noir;
Et qui me nuyst, croy qu'il m'ayde a povoir;
Bourde, verté, au jour d'uy m'est tout un;
Je retiens tout, rien ne sçay concepvoir,
Bien recueully, debouté de chascun.

Prince clement, or vous plaise sçavoir
Que j'entens moult et n'ay sens ne sçavoir:
Parcial suis, a toutes loys commun.
Que fais je plus? Quoy? Les gaiges ravoir,
Bien recueully, debouté de chascun.

VIII — EPITRE A MARIE D'ORLÉANS[170]

Jam nova progenies
celo demittitur alto[171]

I   O louee conception
Envoiee ça jus des cieulx,
Du noble lis[172] digne syon,
Don de Jhesus tres precieulx,
MARIE, nom tres gracieulx,
Fons de pitié, source de grace,
La joye, confort de mes yeulx,
Qui nostre paix bastist et brasse!

II   La paix, c'est assavoir, des riches,
Des povres le substantement,
Le rebours des felons et chiches,
Tres necessaire enfantement,
Conceu, porté honnestement,
Hors le pechié originel,
Que dire je puis sainctement
Souvrain bien de Dieu eternel!

III   Nom recouvré, joye de peuple,
Confort des bons, de maulx retraicte;
Du doulx seigneur premiere et seule
Fille, de son cler sang extraicte,
Du dextre costé Clovis traicte;
Glorieuse ymage en tous fais,
Ou hault ciel creee et pourtraicte
Pour esjouÿr et donner paix!

white swan is nothing but black crow;
he who harms me does his best to help;
lies, truth are now the same to me;
I remember all, but can conceive of nothing,
well received, rebuffed by all.   30

Most clement prince, may you be pleased to know
that much I understand, but have no sense or reason;
I'm strongly partisan and yet agree with all.
What can I do? What? Redeem my things in pawn,
well received, rebuffed by all.   35

VIII — EPISTLE TO MARIE D'ORLÉANS*

*Already a new progeny is sent
down from the high heavens.* *

O blessed birth
sent here below from Heaven,
worthy scion of the noble Lily,
precious gift from Jesus,
Marie, of gracious name,
fount of pity, source of mercy,
joy and comfort of my eyes
who builds and brings about our peace!*   8

The peace, that is, of rich men
and the sustenance of poor,
the stemming of the false and miserly,
O needful childbirth,
conceived and carried honorably
without the sin of Adam,
and therefore can I call it
sovereign good of God Eternal!   16

O name recovered, joy of people,
comfort of the good, shield from evil;
first and only daughter of that gentle
lord, sprung from his clear blood,
from Clovis' right side,
O image glorious in every way,
created and designed in Heaven
for rejoicing and giving peace.   24

145

IV   En l'amour et crante de Dieu
Es nobles flan Cesar conceue,
Des petis et grans en tout lieu
A tres grande joye receue,
D l'amour Dieu traicte, tissue,
Pour les discordez ralier
Et aux enclos donner yssue,
Leurs lians et fers deslier.

V   Aucunes gens, qui bien peu sentent,
Nourris en simplesse et confis,
Contre le vouloir Dieu attentent,
Par ignorance desconfis,
Desirans que feussiez ung fils;
Mais qu'ainsi soit, ainsi m'aist Dieux,
Je croy que ce soit grans proufis.
Raison: Dieu fait tout pour le mieulx.

VI   Du Psalmiste je prens les dis:
Delectasti me, Domine,
In factura tua, si dis:[173]
Noble enfant, de bonne heure né,
A toute doulceur destiné,
Manne du Ciel, celeste don,
De tout bienfait le guerdonné,
Et de noz maulx le vray pardon!

(DOUBLE BALLADE)

Combien que j'ay leu en ung dit:
Inimicum putes, y a,
Qui te presentem laudabit,[174]
Toutesfois, non obstant cela,
Oncques vray homme ne cela
En son courage aucun grant bien,
Qui ne le montrast ça et la:
On doit dire du bien le bien.

Conceived in love and fear of God
and in the noble flanks of Caesar,
received with greatest joy by great
and humble men in every place,
drawn from love of God, woven
for appeasement of discord,
and to free those men imprisoned
and burst their bonds and shackles.   32

Some, understanding little,
nourished in simplicity and confidence,
crippled by their ignorance,
try to undermine the Will of God,
desiring that it were a son;
but being thus, God help me,
I believe it to have been a boon,
for all God's works are for the best.   40

From the Psalmist I take the words:
"For Thou, Lord," he says, "through
Thy work hast made me glad."
O noble child, born beneath a star
of fortune, destined for all sweetness,
manna from Heaven, celestial gift,
recompense for all good works,
and true reprieve from all our ills.*   48

(DOUBLE BALLADE)

Although I've read a saying,
"Consider as your enemy him
who in your presence praises you,"
however and in spite of this,
no true man has hidden
such good fortune in his heart
who did not somehow show it:
one must speak well of good.*   56

Saint Jehan Baptiste ainsy le fist,
Quant l'Aignel de Dieu descela.
En ce faisant pas ne mesfist,
Dont sa voix es tourbes vola;
De quoy saint Andry Dieu loua,
Qui de lui cy ne sçavoit rien,
Et au Fils de Dieu s'aloua:
On doit dire du bien le bien.

Envoiee de Jhesuschrist
Rappeller ça jus par deça
Les povres que Rigueur proscript
Et que Fortune betourna.
Si sçay bien comment il m'en va:
De Dieu, de vous, vie je tien.
Benoist celle qui vous porta!
On doit dire du bien le bien.

Cy, devant Dieu, fais congnoissance
Que creature feusse morte,
Ne feust vostre doulce naissance,
En charité puissant et forte,
Qui ressuscite et reconforte
Ce que Mort avoit prins pour sien;
Vostre presence me conforte:
On doit dire du bien le bien.

Cy vous rans toute obeÿssance,
A ce faire Raison m'exorte,
De toute ma povre puissance;
Plus n'est deul qui me desconforte,
N'aultre ennuy de quelconque sorte.
Vostre je suis et non plus mien;
A ce Droit et Devoir m'enhorte:
On doit dire du bien le bien.

O grace et pitié tres immense,
L'entree de paix et la porte,
Some de benigne clemence,
Qui noz faultes toult et supporte,
Se de vous louer me deporte,
Ingrat suis, et je le maintien,
Dont en ce refrain me transporte:
On doit dire du bien le bien.

Thus did John the Baptist do
when he made known the Lamb of God.
In this he did no wrong,
he whose voice swayed crowds
and made Saint Andrew, who
knew nothing of Him, praise the Lord
and become disciple of His Son:
one must speak well of good.   **64**

O birth sent by Jesus Christ
to this world below as comfort
for the poor proscribed by Harshness
and by Fate maltreated.
I know too well it is through God
and you that I am now alive.
Blest is she who bore you!
One must speak well of good.   **72**

Here, in front of God, I acknowledge
I would have been a creature dead
if not for your sweet birth,
so firm and strong in charity,
which revives and comforts
that which Death had made his own.
Your presence gives me solace:
one must speak well of good.   **80**

To you I hereby swear obedience
(Reason urges me to do this)
to the utmost of my poor power;
no more will grief or any other
trouble now disturb me.
I am yours—no longer mine;
Right and Duty demand this of me:
one must speak well of good.   **88**

O grace and pity so immense,
gate and entrance unto peace,
essence of benignest mercy
which endures and takes away
our faults, if I abstain from praise,
I say that I am then ungrateful,
and so I'm brought to this refrain:
one must speak well of good.   **96**

Princesse, ce loz je vous porte,
Que sans vous je ne feusse rien.
A vous et a tous m'en rapporte:
On doit dire du bien le bien.

VII   Euvre de Dieu, digne, louee
Autant que nulle creature,
De tous biens et vertus douee,
Tant d'esperit que de nature
Que de ceulx qu'on dit d'adventure,
Plus que rubis noble ou balais;
Selon de Caton l'escripture:
Patrem insequitur proles.[174]

VIII   Port asseuré, maintien rassiz,
Plus que ne peut nature humaine,
Et eussiez des ans trente six;
Enfance en rien ne vous demaine.
Que jour ne le die et sepmaine
Je ne sçay qui le me deffant.
A ce propos ung dit ramaine:
De saige mere saige enfant.

IX   Dont resume ce que j'ay dit:
Nova progenies celo,
Car c'est du poëte le dit,
Jamjam demittitur alto.[175]
Saige Cassandre, belle Echo,
Digne Judith, caste Lucresse,
Je vous cognois, noble Dido,
A ma seule dame et maistresse.

X   En priant Dieu, digne pucelle,
Qu'il vous doint longue et bonne vie;
Qui vous ayme, ma damoiselle,
Ja ne coure sur luy envie.
Entiere dame et assouvie,
J'espoir se vous servir ainçoys,
Certes, se Dieu plaist, que devie
Vostre povre escolier FRANÇOYS.

Princess, this praise I bring for you:
without you I would have been as nothing.
And so I state to you and everyone:
one must speak well of good.   100

Work of God, worthy, blessed
as much as any other creature,
gifted with all good and virtue,
as much in spirit and in nature
as those of whom it's said
they're nobler, finer than a ruby.
As Cato wrote, "The offspring
follows in the father's steps."*   108

Port of safety, sustenance
of more than human nature,
even if your age were thirty-six;
you are as if no more a child.
Who is there to hold me back
from speaking thus on any day or week?
I recall a proverb on this matter:
from wise mother, wise child.   116

So I resume what I have said:
"Already a new progeny,"
thus the poet speaks,
"is sent from highest heaven."
O wise Cassandra, lovely Echo,
worthy Judith, chaste Lucretia,
I acknowledge you, O noble Dido,
as my only dame and mistress.*   124

I pray to God, O worthy maiden,
that he may give you long, good life,
and that he who cares for you,
my damsel, suffer not from envy.
O pure and perfect lady,
I hope that I may serve you,
yes, if it please God, before
François, your humble scholar, dies.   132

IX — EPISTRE[176]

(à ses amis)

Aiez pitié, aiez pitié de moy,
A tout le moins, si vous plaist, mes amis!
En fosse gis, non pas soubz houx ne may,
En cest exil ouquel je suis transmis
Par Fortune, comme Dieu l'a permis.
Filles, amans, jeunes gens et nouveaulx,
Danceurs, saulteurs, faisans les piez de veaux,
Vifz comme dars, agus comme aguillon,
Gousiers tintans cler comme cascaveaux,
Le lesserez la, le povre Villon?

Chantres chantans a plaisance, sans loy,
Galans rians, plaisans en fais et dis,
Coureux alans, francs de faulx or, d'aloy,
Gens d'esperit, ung petit estourdis,
Trop demourez, car il meurt entandis.
Faiseurs de laiz, de motetz et rondeaux,
Quant mort sera, vous lui ferez chaudeaux![177]
Ou gist, il n'entre escler ne tourbillon:
De murs espoix on lui a fait bandeaux.
Le lesserez la, le povre Villon?

Venez le veoir en ce piteux arroy,
Nobles hommes, francs de quart et de dix,
Qui ne tenez d'empereur ne de roy,
Mais seulement de Dieu de Paradis:
Jeuner lui fault dimenches et merdis,[178]
Dont les dens a plus longues que ratteaux;
Après pain sec, non pas après gasteaux,
En ses boyaulx verse eaue a gros bouillon;[179]
Bas en terre, table n'a ne tresteaulx.
Le lesserez la, le povre Villon?

Princes nommez, ancïens, jouvenceaux,
Impetrez moy graces et royaulx seaux,
Et me montez en quelque corbillon.
Ainsi le font, l'un a l'autre, pourceaux,
Car, ou l'un brait, ilz fuyent a monceaux.
Le lesserez la, le povre Villon?

IX — EPISTLE*
(*to his Friends*)

Have mercy, have mercy on me,
you my friends at least, if it so please you!
I lie in a ditch, not under holly or green boughs,
in this exile into which I have been sent
by Fate, according to God's will.
Girls, lovers, youths and boys, dancers,
tumblers, those who do the Calf's Foot Step,
as swift as darts, as sharp as spurs,
those whose gullets ring like bells,
will you leave him there, your Poor Villon?   10

Singers singing at your pleasure, without rules,
laughing gallants who so excel in word and deed,
ambling gadflies with no francs of gold or counterfeit,
men of wit, you who sometimes are so scatterbrained,
don't wait too long, for meanwhile he is dying.
Those of you who write motets, rondeaux and lays,
when he is dead, you'll make hot soups for him!
Where he is lying, neither wind nor lightning enter:
thick walls are like a bandage for his eyes.
Will you leave him there, your poor Villon?*   20

Come and see him in this piteous state,
noble men who pay no taxes, and hold
no fief from king or emperor,
but only from our Lord in Heaven.
He's forced to fast on Sundays and Tuesdays,
and now his teeth are longer than a rake's;
after dry bread (no, not after cakes)
he washes out his gut with streams of water;
he lies down on the ground and has no bed or table.
Will you leave him there, your poor Villon?*   30

Princes named above, young and old,
obtain for me the royal grace and seal
and raise me up in some big basket;
pigs do this for one another, for when
one squeaks the others come in droves.
Will you leave him there, your poor Villon?   36

X — REQUESTE A MONSEIGNEUR DE BOURBON[180]

Le mien seigneur et prince redoubté,
Fleuron de lys,[181] royalle geniture,
Françoys Villon, que Travail a dompté
A coups orbes, par force de bature,
Vous supplie par ceste humble escripture
Que lui faciez quelque gracieux prest.
De s'obliger en toutes cours est prest,
Si ne doubtez que bien ne vous contente:
Sans y avoir dommaige n'interest,
Vous n'y perdrez seulement que l'attente.

A prince n'a ung denier emprunté,
Fors a vous seul, vostre humble creature.
De six escus que luy avez presté,
Cela pieça il meist en nourriture.
Tout se paiera ensemble, c'est droiture,
Mais ce sera legierement et prest;
Car, se du glan rencontre en la forest
D'entour Patay, et chastaignes ont vente,[182]
Paié serez sans delay ny arrest:
Vous n'y perdrez seulement que l'attente.

Se je peusse vendre de ma santé
A ung Lombart, usurier par nature,
Faulte d'argent m'a si fort enchanté
Que j'en prendroie, ce cuide, l'adventure.
Argent ne pens a gippon n'a sainture;
Beau sire Dieux! je m'esbaïs que c'est
Que devant moy croix ne se comparoist,
Si non de bois ou pierre, que ne mente;
Mais s'une fois la vraye m'apparoist,[183]
Vous n'y perdrez seulement que l'attente.

Prince du lys, qui a tout bien complaist,
Que cuidez vous comment il me desplaist,
Quant je ne puis venir a mon entente?
Bien m'entendez; aidez moy, s'il vous plaist:
Vous n'y perdrez seulement que l'attente.

X – REQUEST TO THE DUKE OF BOURBON*

My lord and dreaded prince,
fleur-de-lis of royal birth,
François Villon, whom Suffering has stunned
with blows and endless thrashings,
begs you in this humble letter
to make him some gracious loan.
He's ready to engage himself before all courts
of law, so have no fear that he will fail you:
without necessity to bring a suit against him,
your only loss would be in waiting.*   10

He, your humble creature, has borrowed
not a single penny from any prince save you.
Those six *écus* that you once lent him
long since have gone for nourishment.
All at once it will be payed (that's only just)
and yet with speed and promptness;
for if I find some gleanings in the forest
near Patay, and chestnuts are selling well,
you shall be paid without delay or hindrance.
Your only loss would be in waiting.*   20

So much have I been haunted by a lack of money,
that if I now could sell my health
to a Lombard (they're all born usurers),
I think that I would take the chance.
I never carry money in my coat or belt;
good Lord, I am amazed that never
does a cross appear before me
except of stone or wood, to tell the truth;
but if the true cross once would show itself,
your only loss would be in waiting.*   30

Prince of the Lily, in whom good has found perfection,
have you thought how much unhappiness I get
from projects always unfulfilled?
You understand me. Help me, please:
your only loss would be in waiting.   35

Au dos de la lettre

Allez, lettres, faictes ung sault,
Combien que n'ayez pié ne langue,
Remonstrez en vostre harangue
Que faulte d'argent si m'assault.

XI – LE DEBAT DU CUER ET DU CORPS
DE VILLON[184]

Qu'est ce que j'oy?—Ce suis je!—Qui?—Ton cuer,
Qui ne tient mais qu'a ung petit filet:
Force n'ay plus, substance ne liqueur,
Quant je te voy retraict ainsi seulet
Com povre chien tapy en reculet.
Pour quoy est-ce? Pour ta folle plaisance.—
Que t'en chault il?—J'en ay la desplaisance.—
Laisse m'en paix! Pour quoy? J'y penseray.—
Quant sera-ce?—Quant seray hors d'enfance.—
Plus ne t'en dis.—Et je m'en passeray.

Que penses-tu?—Estre homme de valeur.—
Tu as trente ans.—C'est l'aage d'ung mullet.—
Est-e enfance?—Nennil.—C'est donc folleur
Qui te saisist.—Par ou? Par le collet?—
Rien ne congnois.—Si fais, mouches en laict;
L'ung est blanc, l'autre est noir, c'est difference.—[185]
Est-ce donc tout?—Que veulx-tu que je tance?
Se n'est assez je recommenceray.—
Tu es perdu.—J'y mettray resistance.—
Plus ne t'en dis.—Et je m'en passeray.

J'en ay le dueil; toy, le mal et douleur.
Se feusses ung povre ydiot et folet,
Encore eusses de t'excuser couleur:
Si n'as tu soing, tout t'est ung, bel ou let.
Ou la teste as plus dure qu'ung jalet,
Ou mieulx te plaist qu'onneur ceste meschance!
Que respondras a ceste consequence?—
J'en seray hors quant je trespassery.—
Dieu, quel confort!—Quelle sage eloquence!—
Plus ne t'en dis.—Et je m'en passeray.

On the Back of the Letter

Go, my letters, make a leap,
although you have no feet or tongue,
and make it clear in your harangue
that lack of money plagues me.   39

XI – VILLON'S DIALOGUE WITH HIS HEART*

"What do I hear?"—*"It's me."*—"Who?"—*"Your heart*
which hangs on only by a slender thread.
My strength ebbs, my vital sap is drained
when I see you so withdrawn and lonely
like some poor dog crouching in a corner.
And why is that? Because you lead a madcap life."—
"What difference does it make?"—*"I get the worst of it."*—
"Leave me alone! Why, you ask? I'll think about it."—
"When will that be?"—"When my childhood's over."—
"I say no more."—"That's quite alright with me."   10

"What's your intent?"—"To be a man of merit."—
"You're thirty years of age."—"Just like a mule."—
"Is that still childhood?"—"No."—*"Then madness*
has got hold of you."—"Hold of what? My collar?"—
"You don't know a thing."—"Yes I do: flies in milk.
The difference is that one is black and one is white."—
"Is that all?"—"You still want me to argue?
If that is not enough I'll start again."—
"You're lost!"—"I'll try to straighten out."—
"I say no more."—"That's quite alright with me."*   20

"From this I get the sorrow, you the harm and pain.
If you had been some poor mad fool, then
I might have had some reason for excusing you;
but you don't care: good and bad are all the same to you.
It's either that your head is hard as rock,
or else you like misfortune more than honor.
What can you answer to this argument?"—
"I'll be above it when I pass away."—*"God, what*
consolation!"—"What wisdom and what eloquence!"—
"I say no more."—"That's quite alright with me."   30

Dont vient ce mal?—Il vient de mon maleur.
Quant Saturne[186] me feist mon fardelet,
Ces maulx y meist, je le croy.—C'est foleur:
Son seigneur es, et te tiens son varlet.
Voy que Salmon escript en son rolet:[187]
« Homme sage, ce dit il, a puissance
Sur planetes et sur leur influence. »—
Je n'en croy riens; tel qu'ilz m'ont fait seray.—
Que dis tu?—Dea! certes, c'est ma creance.—
Plus ne t'en dis.—Et je m'en passeray.

Veulx tu vivre?—Dieu m'en doint la puissance!—
Il te fault...—Quoy?—Remors de conscience,
Lire sans fin.—En quoy?—Lire en science,
Laisser les folz!—Bien j'y adviseray.—
Or le retien!—J'en ay bien souvenance.—
N'atens pas tant que tourne a desplaisance
Plus ne t'en dis.—Et je m'en passeray.

XII — PROBLEME

(*au nom de la Fortune*)

Fortune fus par clers jadis nommee,
Que toy, Françoys, crie et nomme murtriere,
Qui n'es homme d'aucune renommee.
Meilleur que toy fais user en plastriere,
Par povreté, et fouÿr en carriere;
S'a honte vis, te dois tu doncques plaindre?
Tu n'es pas seul; si ne te dois complaindre.
Regarde et voy de mes fais de jadis,
Mains vaillans homs par moy mors et roidis;
Et n'es, ce sçais, envers eulx ung souillon.
Appaise toy, et mets fin en tes dis.
Par mon conseil prens tout en gré, Villon!

"Whence come these ills?"—"They come from my bad luck.
When Saturn packed my bag for me,
he put them in, I think."—*"That's foolishness.
You are his lord and feel yourself his servant.
Look what Solomon has written in his scroll:
'A wise man,' he says, 'has power
over planets and their influence.'"*—
"I don't believe it; as they've made me, thus I'll be."—
"What did you say?"—"Yes, this is my belief."
"I say no more."—"That's quite alright with me."＊   40

"You want to live?"—"God give me strength to do so!"—
"You then must. . ."—"What?"—*"Feel penitent and read
unceasingly."*—"What sort of things?"—*"Graver subjects,
and leave your foolish friends."*—"I'll think about it."—
"Now don't forget."—"I've made a note of it."—
*"Don't wait so long that things get worse.
I say no more."*—"That's quite alright with me."   47

XII — PROBLEM

(*in the Name of Fortune*)

Scholars gave me, long ago, the name of Fortune,
and you, François, call me a murderer,
you, a man who has no fame at all.
Better men than you, through poverty, I've put
to making plaster or to digging stones in quarries;
so if you live in shame, have you the right to grumble?
You're not alone, so I don't have to pity you.
Look and see what I have done in years gone by:
so many valiant men through me are dead and stiff,
and as you know, compared to them you're nothing
but a kitchen-boy. Calm down and stop this talk.
So learn to take things in your stride, Villon!   12

159

Contre grans roys me suis bien anymee,
Le temps qui est passé ça en arriere:
Priam occis et toute son armee,
Ne luy valut tour, donjon, ne barriere;
Et Hannibal demoura il derriere?
En Cartaige par Mort le feis attaindre;
Et Scypion l'Affriquan feis estaindre;
Julles Cesar au Senat je vendis;
En Egipte Pompee je perdis;
En mer noyé Jason en ung bouillon;
Et une fois Romme et Rommains ardis.
Par mon conseil prens tout en gré, Villon!

Alixandre, qui tant feist de hemee,
Qui voulut veoir l'estoille pouciniere,
Sa personne par moy fut envlimee;
Alphasar roy,[188] en champ, sur sa baniere
Rué jus mort. Cela est ma maniere,
Ainsi l'ay fait, ainsi le maintendray:[189]
Autre cause ne raison n'en rendray.
Holofernes l'ydolastre mauldis,
Qu'occist Judith (et dormoit entandis!)
De son poignart, dedens son pavillon;
Absalon, quoy? en fuyant le pendis.
Par mon conseil prens tout en gré, Villon!

Pour ce, Françoys, escoute que te dis:
Se riens peusse sans Dieu de Paradis,
A toy n'autre ne demourroit haillon,
Car, pour ung mal, lors j'en feroye dix.
Par mon conseil prens tout en gré, Villon!

XIII – QUATRAIN

Je suis Françoys, dont il me poise,
Né de Paris emprès Pontoise,[190]
Et de la corde d'une toise
Sçaura mon col que mon cul poise.

Against great kings I've raised myself,
in days which now are long gone by.
I murdered Priam and his whole army; his towers,
walls and dungeons were no use to him.
Did I spare Hannibal? In Carthage
I made sure that Death caught up with him;
and Scipio Africanus was killed in violence;
I delivered Julius Caesar to the Senate,
and in Egypt brought on Pompey's ruin;
in a whirlpool I had Jason drowned;
and burned both Rome and Romans once.
So learn to take things in your stride, Villon!   24

And Alexander, who fought so many battles
and wished to see the Pleiades,
was poisoned later on by me;
the king Arphaxad I threw down dead
upon his banner. That is my way;
thus I did and thus I shall do;
no other cause or reason must I give.
I put a curse on Holofernes the idolater,
whom Judith slew with his own knife
while he was sleeping inside his tent.
And Absalom? I hanged him as he fled.
So learn to take things in your stride, Villon!*   36

Now listen to what I say, François:
if I could do my will without God's sanction,
I'd leave no rag to you or any man;
for every ill I would return six more,
so learn to take things in your stride, Villon!   41

XIII – QUATRAIN

I am François, which is unfortunate,
born in Paris near Pontoise,
and with a six-foot stretch of rope,
my neck will know my arse's weight.*

XIV – L'EPITAPHE VILLON
(*Ballade des pendus*)

Freres humains qui après nous vivez,
N'ayez les cuers contre nous endurcis,
Car, se pitié de nous povres avez,
Dieu en aura plus tost de vous mercis.
Vous nous voiez cy attachez cinq, six:
Quant de la chair, que trop avons nourrie,
Elle est pieça devorée et pourrie,
Et nous, les os, devenons cendre et pouldre.
De nostre mal personne ne s'en rie;
Mais priez Dieu que tous nous vueille absouldre!

Se freres vous clamons, pas n'en devez
Avoir desdaing, quoy que fusmes occis
Par justice. Toutesfois, vous sçavez
Que tous hommes n'ont pas bon sens rassis;
Excusez nous, puis que sommes transsis,
Envers le fils de la Vierge Marie,
Que sa grace ne soit pour nous tarie,
Nous preservant de l'infernale fouldre.
Nous sommes mors, ame ne nous harie;
Mais priez Dieu que tous nous vueille absouldre!

La pluye nous a debuez et lavez,
Et le soleil dessechiez et noircis;
Pies, corbeaulx, nous ont les yeux cavez,
Et arrachié la barbe et les sourcis.
Jamais nul temps nous ne sommes assis;
Puis ça, puis la, comme le vente varie,
A son plaisir sans cesser nous charie,
Plus becquetez d'oiseaulx que dez a couldre.
Ne soiez donc de nostre confrairie;
Mais priez Dieu que tous nous vueille absouldre!

Prince Jhesus, qui sur tous a maistrie,
Garde qu'Enfer n'ait de nous seigneurie:
A luy n'ayons que faire ne que souldre.
Hommes, icy n'a point de mocquerie;
Mais priez Dieu que tous nous vueille absouldre!

XIV — VILLON'S EPITAPH
(*Ballade of the Hanged*)

Brother men who after us live on,
harden not your hearts against us,
for if you have some pity on us poor men,
the sooner God will show you mercy.
You see us, five, six, strung up here:
as for our flesh, which we have fed too well,
already it has been devoured and is rotten,
and we, the bones, now turn to dust and ashes.
Let no one laugh at all our miseries,
but pray to God that He absolve us all.   10

If we dare call you brothers, you should not
be scornful, even though we have been killed
by justice. All the same, you know
that not all men are wise and strong;
commend us, now that we are dead,
to Jesus, Son of Virgin Mary,
that His grace's source shall not dry up for us,
and that He keep us from the thunderbolts of Hell.
We now are dead—let no one harry us,
but pray to God that He absolve us all.   20

The rain has washed and cleansed us,
and the sun dried and blackened us;
magpies and crows have hollowed out our eyes
and torn away our beards and eyebrows.
Never, never are we at rest,
but driven back and forth
by the wind, changing at its pleasure, we,
more pecked by birds than a tailor's thimble.
Be not of such a brotherhood as ours,
but pray to God that He absolve us all.   30

Prince Jesus, master of us all,
let Hell not hold us in its sway;
we would have no debts or business there.
Men, here there is no joking,
but pray to God that He absolve us all.   35

XV – LOUENGE A LA COURT
DE PARLEMENT[191]

Tous mes cinq sens: yeulx, oreilles et bouche,
Le nez, et vous, le sensitif aussi;
Tous mes membres ou il y a reprouche,
En son endroit ung chascun die ainsi:
« Souvraine Court, par qui sommes icy,
Vous nous avez gardé de desconfire.
Or la langue seule ne peut souffire
A vous rendre souffisantes louenges;
Si parlons tous, fille du souvrain Sire,[192]
Mere des bons et seur des benois anges! »

Cuer, fendez vous, ou percez d'une broche,
Et ne soyez, au moins, plus endurcy
Qu'au desert fut la forte bise roche
Dont le peuple des Juifs fut adoulcy:[193]
Fondez lermes et venez a mercy;
Comme humble cuer qui tendrement souspire,
Louez la Court, conjointe au Saint Empire,[194]
L'eur des François, le confort des estranges,
Procreee lassus ou ciel empire,
Mere des bons et seur des benois anges!

Et vous, mes dens, chascune si s'esloche;
Saillez avant, rendez toutes mercy,
Plus hautement qu'orgue, trompe, ne cloche,
Et de maschier n'ayez ores soussy;
Considerez que je feusse transsy,
Foye, pommon et rate, qui respire;
Et vous, mon corps, qui vil estes et pire
Qu'ours, ne pourceau qui fait son nyt es fanges,
Louez la Court, avant qu'il vous empire,
Mere des bons et seur des benois anges!

Prince, trois jours ne vueillez m'escondire,
Pour moy pourveoir et aux miens « a Dieu » dire;
Sans eulx argent je n'ay, icy n'aux changes.
Court triumphant, *fiat*, sans me desdire,
Mere des bons et seur des benois anges!

XV – PANEGYRIC TO THE
COURT OF PARLIAMENT*

All my five senses—sight, sound, taste,
and smell, and you too, my sense of touch,
all those members branded with disgrace,
each in his own way speaks thus:
"Most Sovereign Court, by grace of whom
we're here, you kept us all from perishing.
And now the tongue alone is not enough
to bestow on you sufficient praise; and so
we all speak, Daughter of our Sovereign Lord,
Mother of the Good, Sister of the Blessed Angels."*   10

O heart, break or pierce yourself with steel,
and be not, at the very least, as hard
as was the strong, gray desert rock
by which the Jewish people were appeased:
melt into tears and cry for mercy;
like a heart that's humble sighing tenderly,
praise the Court, descended from the Emperors,
fortune of the French, defense of foreigners,
born in highest firmament of Heaven,
Mother of the Good, Sister of the Blessed Angels.*   20

And you, my teeth, shake loose,
jump up and all give thanks
more loudly than an organ, bell or trumpet,
and give no longer any thought to chewing;
remember that I would now be dead, along with
liver, lungs and spleen which keep me going;
and you, my body, vile and worse than that
of bear or pig who makes his nest in mud,
praise the Court, before worse things arrive,
Mother of the Good, Sister of the Blessed Angels.   30

Prince, do not deny me three days' grace
to get prepared and say goodby to all my family:
without their help I have no money anywhere.
Triumphant Court, I pray you grant me this request,
Mother of the Good, Sister of the Blessed Angels.   35

XVI – QUESTION AU CLERC DU GUICHET[195]
(*Ballade de l'appel*)

Que vous semble de mon appel,
Garnier? Feis je sens ou folie?
Toute beste garde sa pel;
Qui la contraint, efforce ou lie,
S'elle peult, elle se deslie.
Quant donc par plaisir voluntaire
Chantee me fut ceste omelie,[196]
Estoit il lors temps de moy taire?

Se feusse des hoirs Hue Cappel,[197]
Qui fut extrait de boucherie,
On ne m'eust, parmy ce drappel,
Fait boire en ceste escorcherie.
Vous entendez bien joncherie?
Mais quant ceste paine arbitraire
On me jugea par tricherie,
Estoit il lors temps de moy taire?

Cuidiez vous que soubz mon cappel
N'eüst tant de philosophie
Comme de dire: « J'en appel »?
Si avoit, je vous certiffie,
Combien que point trop ne m'y fie.
Quant on me dist, present notaire:
« Pendu serez! » je vous affie,
Estoit il lors temps de moy taire?

Prince, se j'eusse eu la pepie,[198]
Pieça je feusse ou est Clotaire,
Aux champs debout comme une espie.
Estoit il lors temps de moy taire?

XVI – QUESTION TO THE CLERK
OF THE PRISON GATE*
(*Ballade of Appeal*)

What do you think of my appeal,
Garnier? Was it right or wrong?
Every creature watches out for his
own skin; if one gets caught
he tries his best to get away.
So when for no good reason
they preached to me that sermon,
should I have kept my mouth shut, eh?* 16

Now if I was an heir of Hugues Capet,
whose father was a butcher,
the people in the slaughter-house
would not have made me drink
through cloth. You get my meaning?
When they reached in their bag of tricks
and slapped that sentence on me,
should I have kept my mouth shut, eh?* 16

Do you think that underneath
my hat there weren't brains enough
to tell them, "I appeal"?
You bet there were, enough to have
no faith in men like those.
When I was told in front of notaries,
"You will be hanged," I ask you,
should I have kept my mouth shut, eh? 24

Prince, if I had been struck dumb,
I would have been where Clotaire is,
or strung up like a dirty spy.
Should I have kept my mouth shut, eh?* 28

Le Jargon et Jobelin / Poems in Slang

LE JARGON ET JOBELIN

I

A Parouart, la grant mathe gaudie
Ou accolez sont duppez et noirciz,
Et par les anges suivans la paillardie
Sont greffiz et prinz cinq ou six;
La sont befleurs au plus haut bout assis
Pour l'evagie, et bien haut mis au vent.
Eschequez moy tost ces coffres massis:
Car vendengeurs des ances circuncis[199]
S'en brouent du tout a neant.
Eschec, eschec pour le fardis!

Brouez moy sur ces gours passans,
Avisez moy bien tost le blanc,
Et pietonnez au large sus les champs
Qu'au mariage ne soyez sur le banc
Plus qu'un sac n'est de plastre blanc.
Se gruppez estes des carieux,
Rebignez moy tost ces enterveux
Et leur monstrez des trois le bris
Qu'enclavés no soiés deux et deux:
Eschec, eschec pour le fardis!

Plantez aux hurmes vos picons.
De paour des bisans si tres durs,
Et aussi d'estre sur les joncs
Enmahés en coffres en gros murs,
Escharicés, ne soiez point durs,
Que le grant Can ne vous face essorez.
Songears ne soiez pour dorer,
Et babignez tousjours aux ys
Des sires pour les desbouser.
Eschec, eschec pour le fardis!

POEMS IN SLANG

I

In Paris, on that hill where fools
are hung and blackened in the wind,
and where cops, all grifters themselves,
string up five or six at once,
there they put the con-men up on top
so they can feel the nice cool breeze.
Stay clear of thick-walled cells, because
a cutpurse with his ears chopped off
is about as good as done for.
Watch out for guys like hangmen.*   10

Jump rich men passing by,
find out how much cash they've got,
then hit the open road, so they
won't stick you on that scaffold
that's whiter than a sack of plaster.
If those cops catch sight of you,
stay on the ball and let them
only see your ass; that way
they won't clap you into irons.
Watch out for guys like hangmen.   20

Avoid those hooks they hang the noose from.
If you don't want to feel that rough north wind
or sack-out on a pile of straw
in a grimy cell inside thick walls,
take off and don't be too thick-skulled;
that way the provost won't have you drying
in the breeze. Have the guts to cheat
and fill the ears of jerks with lies
so you can fleece them.
Watch out for guys like hangmen.   30

Prince froart dis arques petis,
L'un des sires si ne soit endormis.
Luez au bec que ne soiés greffis
Et que vos emps n'en aient du pis:
Eschec, eschec pour le fardis.

II

Coquillars enarvans a Ruel,
Men ys vous chante que gardés
Que n'y laissez corps et pel.
Qu'on fist de Collin l'Escailler[200]
Devant la roe babiller;
Il babigna pour son salut.
Pas ne sçavoit oignons peler,
Dont l'amboureux luy rompt le suc.

Changés vos andosses souvent,
Et tirés tout droit au temple;[201]
Et eschiqués tost, en brouant,
Qu'en la jarte no soiez emple.
Montigny[202] y fut par exemple
Bien attaché au halle grup
Et y jargonnast il le tremple,
Dont l'amboureux luy rompt le suc.

Gailleurs faitz en piperie
Pour ruer les ninars au loing,
A la sault tost, sans suerie!
Que les mignons ne soient au gaing
Farcis d'ung plumbis a coing[203]
Qui griffe au gart le duc,
Et de la dure si tres loing
Dont l'amboureux luy rompt le suc.

Prince, erriere de Ruel
Et n'eussiez vous denier ne pluc,
Qu'au giffle ne laissez l'appel
Pour l'amboureux qui rompt le suc.

Prince, when you're cracking safes, remember
that some square might not be sleeping;
watch out they don't pick you up
and make things rough for you.
Watch out for guys like hangmen.   35

II

Coquillards who rough guys up,
I tell you to watch out
you don't lose your skin.
They made Colin de Cayeux
sing in front of cops;
he talked to save himself, and didn't
even know enough to con them,
and now the hangman's snapped his neck.*   8

Keep changing outfits
and ducking into churches;
take off—make sure your
clothes don't trip you up.
To show the others
they strung up Montigny;
he babbled to the crowd a while,
and then the hangman snapped his neck.*   16

Knights, masters at the art of conning,
to throw the archers off the scent,
take off fast and don't kill no one.
When the loot's being divied up,
don't let the pretty boys be sitting
with a chunk of lead stuck in their mouth,
on their way to another world
when the hangman snaps their necks.*   24

Prince, stay clear of rough stuff,
and when you're down and out, don't let
appeals get stuck inside your throat,
or else the hangman'll snap your neck.   28

III

Spelicans
Qui en tous temps
Avancez dedans le pogoiz
Gourde piarde,
Et sur la tarde
Desboursez les pauvres nyois;
Et pour soustenir voz pois
Les duppes sont privés de caire,
Sans faire haire
Ne hault braire,
Metz plantez ils sont comme jonz
Par les sires qui sont si longs.

Souvent aux arques
A leurs marques
Se laissent tous desbouses
Pour ruer
Et enterver;
Pour leur contre que lors faisons
La fee aux arques vous respons,
Et rue deux coups ou trois
Aux gallois.
Deux ou trois
Nineront trestous au frontz
Pour les sires qui sont si longs.

Pour ce, bernadz
Coquillars,
Rebecquez vous la montjoye
Qui desvoye
Votre proye
Et vous fera du tout brouer.
Par joncher et enterver,
Qui est aux pigons bien chair,
Pour rifler
Et placquer
Les angels de mal tous rons
Pour les sires qui sont si longs.

III

Picklocks,
  you who always
cram fat fingers way down
  inside pockets,
  and at night
fleece poor suckers who
do everything you say
so you can take their dough,
  and never shout
  for help
but stand rooted to the spot, afraid
of guys who play it rough.   12

Often, in bed
  with whores
they let themselves be fleeced
  so they can keep on
  making love;
us, we suddenly turn up
from down behind some chests
and club them once or twice,
  these lover-boys,
  once or twice
on their thick skulls,
we guys who play it rough.   24

So, dimwit
  Coquillards,
stay clear of gallows
  that'll loosen
  up your ass
and make your guts spill out;
that's where jerks wind up
who spend their time with whores,
  or take
  the lousy
cops and work them over,
like guys who play it rough.   36

De paour des hurmes
  Et des grumes,
Rasurez vous en droguerie
  Et faierie,
Et ne soiez plus sur les joncs
Pour les sires qui sont si longs.

IV

Saupicquez, fronans des gours arques
Pour desbouser beaussire dieux,
Allés ailleurs planter vos marques!
Benards, vous estes rouges gueux;
Berart s'en va chez les joncheux
Et babigne qu'il a plongis.
Mes freres, soiez embraieux,
Et gardez des coffres massis!

Si gruppés estes, desgrappez
De ces angels si graveliffes;
Incontinant manteaulx et chappes
Pour l'emboue ferez eclipses.
De vos farges serés besifles,
Tout debout, nompas assis.
Pour ce, gardés vous d'estre griffés
En ces gros coffres massis.

Niaiz qui seront attrappez
Bien tost s'en brouent au halle;
Plus n'y vault que tost ne happez
La baudrouse de quatre talle:
Destires fait la hirenalle
Quand le gosier est assegis;
Et si hurcque la pirenalle
Au saillir des coffres massis.

Prince des gayeuls les sarpes,
Que vos contres ne soient greffis;
Pour doubte de frouer aux arques,
Gardez vous des coffres massis.

To keep from swinging
  on some rope,
make sure you're good and sharp
  at con-games,
and don't wind up in cells like those
for guys who play it rough.   42

IV

You, the heavies that crack safes
and sweep them clear of cash,
shack up some other place.
You wise-guys aren't so smart;
some rat always goes
and sings in front of cops.
So boys, keep buttoned up,
stay clear of thick-walled cells.   8

If you're caught, shake loose
from those damned cops,
and stash away the clothes you swiped
for fear of getting hung.
That chain they put around your neck
will choke you standing up.
So, be careful you aren't caught
and slapped in thick-walled cells.   16

Jerks who let themselves get caught
soon wind up swinging,
or better yet get flailed
with cat-o-nine tails
(which makes their hair stand up
on end), with a gag stuck
in their mouth, when they
get out of thick-walled cells.   24

Prince of guys who like good times,
don't let them nab your friends;
for fear of getting scragged in jail,
stay clear of thick-walled cells.   28

V

Joncheurs jonchans en joncherie,
Rebignez bien ou joncherez
Qu'Ostac[204] n'embroue vostre arerie
Ou accolés sont vos ainsnez.
Poussez de la quille et brouez,
Car tost seriez rouppieux.
Eschec que ne soiés acollez
Par la poe du marieux!

Bendez vous contre la faerie
Quant vous auront desbousés,
N'estant a juc la rifflerie
Des angelz et leurs assosés.
Berard, se vous puist, renversez;
Si greffir laissez vos carrieux,
La dure bien tost renversez
Pour la poe du marieux.

Entervez a la floterie;
Chanter leur trois, sans point songer;
Qu'en astes ne soiez en surie
Blanchir vos cuirs et essurger.
Bignés la mathe, sans targer,
Que vos ans n'en soient ruppieux.
Plantez ailleurs contre assieger
Pour la poe du marieux.

Prince benardz en esterie,
Querez couplaus pour ramboureux;
Et autour de vos ys, luezie
Pour la poe du marieux.

V

Con-men conning in confidence,
be careful where you con,
so Ostac won't set your kids
to swinging like your parents.
Shake a leg, take off if you
don't want a snotty nose;
don't let your neck get wrung
by the hangman's filthy paws.* 8

Gang up against the cops
when they try and shake you down;
they don't have to take the rap
for things they swipe from you.
Slug them if you can, because
once those guys get hold of you,
you'll be polished off
by the hangman's filthy paws. 16

Watch out for the law; tell them
all to go to Hell—don't worry;
be careful they don't hang
your hide up in a tannery to dry.
Don't wait around, take off,
don't let your nose get snotted up.
Keep on the move, for fear
of the hangman's filthy paws. 24

Prince of jerks who stick around,
hit the open road, move on,
and always keep your eyes peeled
for the hangman's filthy paws. 28

VI

Contres de la gaudisserie,
Entervez tousjours blanc pour bis,
Et frappez, en la hurterie,
Sur les beaux sires bas assis.
Ruez des feuilles cinq ou six,
Et vous gardés bien de la roe
Qui aux sires plante du gris
En leur faisant faire la moe.

La giffle gardés de rurie,
Que vos corps n'en aient du pis,
Et que point a la turterie
En la hurme ne soiés assis.
Prenez du blanc, laissez le bis,
Ruez par les fondes la poe,
Car le bizac, avoir advis,
Fait aux beroars faire la moe.

Plantez de la mouargie,
puis ça, puis la, pour l'urtis,
Et n'espargnez point la flogie
Des doux dieux sur les patis.
Vos ens soient assez hardis
Pour leur avancer la droe;
Mais soient memoradis
Qu'on ne vous face faire la moe.

Prince, qui n'a bauderie
Pour eschever de la soe,[205]
Danger de grup en arderie,
Fait aux sires faire la moe.

VI

All you guys who like good times,
it's cash you want, not women;
set to work in crowds
on coins way down in pockets—
make fast with wallets.
Stay clear of the law which puts
dumb jerks up where it's breezy
and sets their mouths to twisting.

Don't let them work you over—
that treatment's none too healthy;
don't let them set you swinging
on their little scaffold.
Take cash, forget your women;
stick your fingers inside pockets,
or else that breeze that hits your face
will set your mouth to twisting.

In place of good stuff, every now
and then hand out some cash that's fake.
Don't worry none about those
monks that live out in the sticks;
get up the nerve to palm off
fake stuff on those jerks too.
But don't forget that someone just
might set your mouths to twisting.

Prince, whatever guys aren't smart **enough**
to dodge that bit with boiling oil,
with hooks and fire, it's up to you
to set their mouths to twisting. *

Notes

Notes to THE LEGACY

1. Vegetius was a fourth-century Roman writer, author of a *De re militari*.
2. These two lines contain a series of obscene *double-entendres*. *Planter* and *coignier* normally meant "to plant" and "to mint"; but in the slang of the day they both meant "to copulate". *Complans*, "a plot of ground for cultivation", also had a slang meaning, one which I will leave the reader to surmise.
3. Villon's motives for going to Angers were not quite so innocent as he would have us believe. In the first place he had just, or was about to, help rob the College of Navarre, and thus Paris was soon to become a bit warm for him. Secondly he and his gang seem to have been meditating fleecing an old, rich priest in Angers, and apparently Villon was to go there as their finger-man.
4. A *soret* is a red herring (one which has been cured and dried), for which Boulogne was famous.
5. For Guillaume de Villon, François' protector and the man from whom he took his name, see the biography and *Testament*, lines 849 ff.
6. Tents and pavilions (standards). Villon is here pretending he is a rich knight, bequeathing lordly possessions of great value. Naturally this is all a hoax. The same with the sword in stanza XI, the diamond in XII, the coat of mail in XV, the hundred francs in XVII, and the dogs in XVII and XIX (dogs for hunting were permitted only to noblemen).
7. Ythier Marchand, apparently a boyhood friend of Villon, came from a wealthy Parisian family important in parliamentary circles. Later on he became involved in Burgundian politics to the point where Louis XI said he was the man he most hated. The King finally bought his loyalty, but then he became implicated in a plot to poison

Louis XI and died mysteriously in prison in 1474. (He's also mentioned in the *Testament*, line 970). The *branc* that Villon bequeaths him literally means "short sword", but he probably intended a pun with *bran*, "excrement".

8. Jean le Cornu belonged to a rich family of financiers. In Villon's youth he was in what we would now call the Treasury, and he was later to become civil clerk and then criminal clerk to the Châtelet. He died of the plague in 1476. Villon mentions him again in the *Testament* (line 990) where, depending on how we read those lines, he expresses either gratitude or, sarcastically, tremendous bitterness.

9. Pierre de Saint-Amand was Clerk of the Treasury, a post of great importance then. Since such high government officials were accustomed to ride around Paris on horses or mules, Villon wills him two taverns with appropriate names. He reappears in the *Testament*, line 1007.

10. Jean de Blaru was a goldsmith with a shop on the Pont-au-Change, one of the two bridges connecting the Île-de-la-Cité with the Right Bank of Paris. The gift of a mythical diamond might have been prompted as a sarcastic solution to an actual lawsuit over just such a stone in which Blaru was engaged. The reason for the gift of the "Striped Ass" (or "Zebra"), a common Parisian house-sign, is a mystery.

11. These lines reflect a battle that was then raging between the regular clergy and the University of Paris on the one hand, and the Mendicant Orders on the other. In 1215 the Church had issued the decree *Omnis utriusque sexus* ordering all Christians to confess at least once a year with their parish priest. Then along came the Mendicants who early in the 15th century also received the right from the Pope to hear confessions. This enraged the regular clergy, but in 1449 the Mendicants' right was reaffirmed with the "Carmelite" bull. Villon, whose upbringing had made him a sworn enemy of the Mendicant Friars, bequeaths the seculars their old 1215 decree to hearten them.

12. Master Robert Vallée came from a rich family of financiers and was probably Villon's companion at the University. Calling him a "poor clerk" and offering to buy him a measly scribe's stall are pure sarcasms. From these stanzas one gathers he was somewhat of a blockhead, and furthermore led around by his mistress, who is to receive Villon's breeches (in hock at the *Trumillières*, a tavern near Les Halles), so she can more effectively "wear the pants". The *Art of Memory* was a didactic book quite widely

read in the 15th century, and was sort of a cross between the Synopticon and Dale Carnegie.

13. Jacques Cardon was a rich clothier, who therefore had no need whatsoever of Villon's fictitious gloves and silk cape. The gift of an acorn from a willow grove is equivalent to a gift of nothing. (*Glan* also meant the right to pasture pigs in an oak forest, in which case the line has the same meaning, but with the added tinge of associating Cardon's eating habits with those of said animal.)

14. Regnier de Montigny came from an important but impoverished family. At an early age he turned to the life of a card-shark and crook, and seems to have been the one responsible for introducing Villon to the underworld of the Coquillards. After a long history of scrapes with the law, he was hanged at Paris in 1457, less than a year after Villon wrote these lines.

15. About Jean Raguier we know little more than what Villon himself tells us in lines 1070-1071 of the *Testament*.

16. The Seigneur de Grigny was Philippe Brunel, a violent, quarrelsome nobleman, detested by everyone. Later in life he seems to have attempted to solve his financial problems by robbing his own church of Grigny. As a result he spent fourteen months in prison with intermittent interrogations and torture sessions, and then at the trial he was so irascible and insulting as to make his case hopeless. The tower of Nigeon and the castle of Bicêtre were both in ruins in 1456 when Villon made this fictitious legacy.

17. About Mouton and his lawsuit with Brunel we know nothing more than Villon tells us here. *Chanjon* technically meant "changeling", but at the same time was used as a fairly strong insult.

18. Jacques Raguier was probably the son of Charles VII's master cook, Lubin Raguier, and it was perhaps in the royal kitchens that he developed the truly magnificent ability to absorb liquid refreshment that Villon ascribes to him. The *abreuvoir Popin* was a trough for watering horses near the Seine on the Right Bank. Line 147, like line 124 above, probably means "nothing". The *Pomme de Pin* was a well-known tavern on the Île-de-la-Cité. *Planter* here probably means "to joke, jest", but it also has the meaning discussed above in note 2.

19. Jean Mautaint was Examiner at the Châtelet, and the fellow who, shortly after this was written, was to handle the investigation of the College of Navarre robbery. Pierre Basanier was at this time a notary at the Châtelet, and in the following year was to be made criminal clerk. The

seigneur who punishes disturbances is the Provost, Robert d'Estouteville, who seems to some degree to have been Villon's protector. In any case, as head of the Parisian police, he was an extremely powerful man, and either out of gratitude or fear, Villon's only references to him (here and *Testament*, line 1369) are veiled.

20. Pierre Fournier was not Villon's personal lawyer, as he would like to have us believe, but the attorney who represented the community of Saint-Benoît at the Châtelet.

21. Jean Trouvé was an assistant butcher in the *Grande-Boucherie* of Paris. *Le Mouton, Le Boeuf Couronné,* and *La Vache* which Villon bequeaths him are appropriate house-signs. The latter was in a street called *Troussevache* (Carrycow) in which undoubtedly hung a sign representing a man carrying a cow on his shoulders, a villain which Villon suggests the butcher should try to catch.

22. To understand this bequest, one must realize that the Captain of the Watch, who had to be a knight in order to hold this post, was then Jean de Harlay, whose claims to knighthood (and therefore his right to the job) another man was contesting. Since a helm was a symbol of knighthood, Villon settles the whole issue in one blow by bequeathing him an appropriate tavern-sign. He bequeaths two rubies because they were said to shine in the dark. (There's considerable confusion about the French text here. Half of the sources give instead of *rubis, riblis,* which according to one authority means "affray, scuffle", and according to another "robbery, object robbed". Short of tossing a three-sided coin, it seems hopeless trying to fathom which of these solutions Villon intended.) In *les Troys Lis* there's another Villonesque pun: aside from "lilies", *lis* can also mean "beds", objects which he would have been only too happy to see in the Châtelet dungeons.

23. Pierre Marchand was tipstaff (constable, bailiff) at the Châtelet, and, like law-enforcement officers since time immemorial, not always so eager to enforce the law. Villon accuses him of being a "good merchant", a phrase which then meant "bad egg" or "procurer", which last seems to be the meaning Villon intends here. A propos of the straw in line 180, not only was it used for mattresses, but prostitutes' rooms were strewn with it in those days. If procuring was his only profession when Villon wrote the *Legacy* in 1456, he seems to have become more versatile by the time the *Testament* was written five years later, for there (lines 1098-1099) Villon suggests that he was fairly handy with loaded dice and marked cards.

24. Jean le Loup and Casin Cholet were two badhat friends of Villon who seemed willing to overlook any moral shortcomings of the myriad professions they undertook, as long as they proved remunerative. In addition, their language was none too dainty—it seems that in 1460 they were hauled in for referring to a certain abbess as a "married slut, whore and debauchée". Anyhow, by 1456 they had jobs as river police of the Seine, without anyone knowing who gave them the jobs, and without anyone being able to kick them out. It would appear that Villon joined them in night duck-hunting sessions. He bequeaths them long cloaks presumably the better to hide stolen goods; firewood and charcoal because, since it was their job to prevent people stealing this as it was unloaded from boats, it was what they could most easily appropriate. Boots without tops aren't going to do them much good wading.

25. These two stanzas are pure sarcasm. The *trois petis enfans tous nus*, Colin Laurens, Girart Gossouyn and Jean Marceau (or Marcel) were old duffers, usurers and speculators (chiefly in salt), immensely wealthy and thoroughly detested. In addition Marceau, the richest and most unscrupulous of the three, was the personal enemy of Villon's protector, Robert d'Estouteville. The *blancs* in line 206 were small silver coins; four of them would be equivalent to about a dollar. Line 207, in addition to the meaning I've given, was also a colloquialism meaning, "they'll be six feet under".

26. Villon indulges in similar sarcasms with Guillaume Cotin and Thibaud de Vitry, both of whom were canons of Notre-Dame, old and wealthy, who at one time or another held down important fiscal and judicial posts and who came from families very important in governmental and royal circles. For years Villon's church of Saint-Benoît had been involved in an ecclesiastical quarrel with the chapter of Notre-Dame, which was one more reason for Villon's detesting these old codgers.

The Letter of Nomination from the University showed a graduate's eligibility to be presented for a benefice. Guillot Gueuldry was an insolvent butcher who hadn't payed the rent on his house for years. The crosier (line 225), a symbol of the bishop's office, is what they would have both loved to have; short of that Villon gives them a house-sign by that name.

27. "Pigeon" was a slang word for prisoner and *trappe vollière* (literally "bird-trap") meant prison.

28. In those days glass was a rarity and instead window-frames (*chassis*) were often hung with cloth or paper. Even this is too much for Villon; all he can offer are spiders' webs. The stalls in the next line were outdoor shops that lined many streets in Paris then. Bums would use them as shelter whenever they could.

29. The Mendicant Friars consisted of four orders: the Dominicans (in France, *Jacobins* or *Frères Prêcheurs*), the Franciscans (*Cordeliers* or *Frères Mineurs*), the Carmelites (*Carmes*) and the Augustinians. The *Filles-Dieu* (also called *Dévotes*) were nuns dedicated to the care of the sick, and the *Béguines* were more or less lay nuns—nuns whose vows were not perpetual. The Fifteen Signs are those which precede the Last Judgment; this was a favorite topic of 15th-century preachers.

30. Jean de la Garde was a wealthy, prominent Parisian *épicier*, which in those days did not denote "grocer" as it does today, but rather a seller of spices, and broadly, a man who dealt in any goods from the Levant, even such as cotton and sugar. Most condiments were then ground in mortars, so Villon gives him an appropriate sign and a votive crutch, one left at Saint-Maur by pilgrims cured of the gout, to use as a pestle.

31. Who is being referred to here is a mystery; in addition, the phrase *griefz exploiz* could also refer to legal proceedings (with the context a blank it's impossible to decide which translation to choose). Saint Anthony's Fire was a disease epidemic and common to the period; its modern, and somewhat less expressive, medical name is gangrenous erysipelas.

32. Pierre Merbeuf was a rich clothier of the Rue des Lombards and Nicolas de Louviers was an equally wealthy city magistrate and tax-collector. Gouvieux was a village in ruins near Chantilly, north of Paris. The Prince in the last line is the Prince of Fools who in street processions would distribute cardboard coins in imitation of the King who on similar occasions distributed real ones.

33. The Sorbonne bell, named Marie, was famous and on a calm day could be heard all over Paris. At nine every evening it rang out simultaneously the curfew and the Angelus (*Angelus Domini nuntiavit Mariae*, the Angel of the Lord announced to Mary). Villon's room was less than a hundred feet from the Sorbonne, and so on a cold winter's night the sound of its pealing must have pervaded his little room.

34. These two and a half stanzas are a take-off on the jargon of Scholastic philosophy, which Rabelais said was dis-

puted *Sorbonificabilitudissinement*. Since Villon was more interested here in the ominous sound of thinly gallicized Latin terms than in conveying any heartfelt meaning, I have translated these lines accordingly. The Scholastic "species" (*espèces*) are used to denote the mental faculties, the different varieties of which Villon lists.

35. Thibaud d'Auxigny was the hard, uncompromising bishop of Orléans who had Villon incarcerated in the dungeons of the episcopal palace of Meung (see biography). "Blessing streets" means blessing the people as he passes in a street procession.

36. This is a pun on *serf* ("serf") and *cerf* ("stag"); hence the "doe" following.

37. For Cotart see *Testament*, 1230, and the ballade following.
   The Picards were a heretical sect which rejected the use of prayer; hence, saying a Picard's prayer is equivalent to saying absolutely nothing. Although Lille and Douai are now in France, in those days, as part of the enormous domains of the Duke of Burgundy, they were a part of Flanders, and a branch of this sect seems to have established itself there.

38. This is Psalm 108. Its seventh verse is an appropriate gift, as it reads "Let his days be few, and let another take his bishopric". (In the King James version it is the eighth verse and is differently translated.)

39. This is Louis XI who had become king in 1461. On his passage through Meung Villon had been freed from prison (see the biography), hence the extravagant and slightly embarrassing expression of gratitude which weighs down the next several stanzas.

40. Saint Martial was a third-century bishop of Limoges. Possibly because of a popular etymology, he was accredited with "martial" virtues, none of which he had. The "late Dauphin" is Louis XI, and "late" not in the sense that he has just died, but in the sense that he is no longer Dauphin, but king.

41. *Sans croix ne pille* literally means "without head or tail (of a coin)". In those days one side of coins had a cross imprinted on them. The Gospel passage quoted here is

Luke XXIV, 13-32. The town in line 101 is Moulins, residence of the Duke of Bourbon, and *esperance* ("hope") was the device of the Bourbons.

42. The *Roman de la Rose* is a long allegorical poem written in the thirteenth and early fourteenth centuries by Guillaume de Lorris and Jean de Meung. Aside from *The Golden Legend*, a compilation of the lives of the saints for purely popular consumption, it was the most widely read work of the fourteenth and fifteenth centuries. It's not surprising to find Villon well acquainted with it, and to find references to it scattered throughout his work.

43. The reader is cautioned not to take too seriously Villon's protestations of innocence concerning the squandering of money on such things as food and women.

44. The two quotations in the first stanza are from Ecclesiastes XI, verses 9 and 10. The second stanza is taken from Job VII, 6.

45. The Celestines were and the Carthusians still are religious orders with a preference for eremetical life. The reference to oyster fishermen in the next line is a bit mysterious, but seems to indicate that they dressed and lived rather better than the founders of their orders had intended.

46. "Let's leave the church where it is" was an expression meaning "let's change the topic".

47. Jacques Coeur was without a doubt the most spectacular businessman of the Middle Ages. From relatively humble origins he rose to being one of the wealthiest individuals France has ever seen. He obtained enormously important government posts, including that of master of the mint under Charles VII, and with his own money aided the French government in the latter days of the Hundred Years' War. Finally, after getting a strangle-hold on France's trade and having many members of the court in debt to him for huge sums, he was accused (among other things) of having poisoned the King's mistress. He fled France and while on his way to fight the Turks, died at Chios on the 25th of November, 1456, just one month before Villon wrote *The Legacy*.

48. Psalm 103, verses 15 and 16. The whole passage is: "As for man, his days are as grass: as a flower of the field, so he flourisheth. For the wind passeth over it, and it is gone; and the place thereof shall know it no more."

49. Upturned collars, usually lined with fur were a 15th-century woman's fashion. It is curious to note that more than once ordinances were issued prohibiting prostitutes from wearing them, partly in line with religious beliefs forbidding vanities, and partly so that women of the upper

classes, by being the only ones to wear them, could have the comfort of knowing themselves easily distinguishable from prostitutes.

Atours were the conical hats worn by the noblewomen of the day, and *bourrelets* were the fashion for the bourgeoisie—they consisted of a horse-hair lined headdress onto which a hood was affixed.

50. Taking all the names in this famous ballade in order:

Flora was a celebrated Roman courtesan mentioned by Juvenal.

Archipiada baffled scholars for years until one put forward the ingenious theory (now accepted) that Villon was thinking of Alcibiades, whose name he had caught imperfectly in class, whom Boetius mentions as a model of beauty, and who therefore was assumed to be a woman in the less omni-sexual Middle Ages.

Thaïs was the Athenian courtesan who followed Alexander into Egypt (and since made famous by Anatole France and the composer, Massenet).

Echo, Héloïse and Abelard are all three well enough known.

Buridan was not only a famous 14th-century professor at the University of Paris but also the hero of an equally famous legend. When he was a student, it began to be noised about that the Queen of France (and Navarre) was inviting students to her palace bordering on the Seine, giving them fine meals, sleeping with them and then having them tossed to a watery death in the river. Buridan managed to get himself an invitation, and everything the rumors said turned out to be true. For three days they ate, drank, listened to sweet music and made love. Then came his time to be tossed out the window; but Buridan had arranged for a barge full of hay to pass beneath the palace. As he landed in it, his fellow-students guiding the barge dropped a large rock into the river to reassure the Queen.

Being a kill-joy lot, modern scholars have proved that this story is a fabrication. It appears that the Queen in question, Jeanne de Navarre, died when Buridan was about five years old, which, while not making the story impossible, at least makes it improbable.

Queen Blanche was Blanche de Castille, mother of Louis IX.

Big-footed Bertha, Beatrice and Alice are all three heroines of a medieval *Chanson de geste, Hervi de Metz.* The first was the legendary wife of Pépin le Bref and mother of Charlemagne.

Arembourg was heiress of Maine and wife of the somewhat notorious Foulques d'Anjou. She died in 1126.

Joan of Lorraine, of course, is Joan of Arc.

51. Taking the names of this ballade in order:

Calixtus III was pope from 1455 to 1458 when he died.
He was Alfonso de Borgia, and uncle of the infinitely
more notorious Borgia pope, Alexander VI. He was famous in Villon's day for having preached a crusade
against the Turks.

Alfonso V, King of Aragon and Naples, called The
Magnanimous, was a great warrior and patron of the arts.
He too died in 1458.

Charles, Duke of Bourbon, died in 1456 and was the
father of the Duke of Bourbon to whom Villon addressed
his *Request* (Misc. Poems X).

Arthur III, Duke of Britanny and Constable of France,
died in 1458.

Charles VII was King of France from 1422 to 1461.

James II was known as "the kyng of Scotts with the
rede face", and was killed in 1460 by the explosion of a
huge cannon while besieging Roxburgh Castle.

The King of Cyprus was Jean III de Lusignan who
died in 1458.

After the splendid little piece of irony in line 371, it
would be gratuitous pedantry to try to identify the King
of Spain in the preceding line.

Ladislaus, King of Bohemia, died in 1457.

Du Guesclin was constable of France under Charles V
and one of the greatest heroes of the Hundred Years' War.
He died in 1380.

The Dauphin d'Auvergne is probably Béraud III, dead
in 1426.

The "late" Duke d'Alençon is either, by a twist of irony,
Jean II who was not dead when Villon wrote this, but
who had been condemned for treason and dispossessed of
his lands and titles in 1458; or it could be Jean I who died
at the Battle of Agincourt in 1415.

Note that all the people mentioned in this ballade
(except for those of the *envoi*, and the two jokes—the
King of Spain and Ladislaus' grandfather) are not only
contemporaries of Villon, but men who died between 1456
(when he wrote *The Legacy*) and 1461 (when he wrote
The Testament).

52. This ballade is an attempt on Villon's part to write in
Old French, the language of about 250 years earlier. As
scholars love to point out, it is packed full of grammatical

blunders, Villon's knowledge of the language of his ancestors being somewhat dim.

Even though the "noble King of France" in line 395 seems to be Saint Louis, identifying the people mentioned in this ballade would be a more or less irrelevant task, as Villon is purposely being vague, using titles of nobility more as symbols than as designating actual people.

53. The Belle Heaulmière (Beautiful Armoress—see note 54 on the origin of such names as this) in her youth was one of the better known beauties and demi-mondaines of Paris. She was born around 1375, and towards the age of twenty became the mistress of Nicolas d'Orgemont (called "the Lame"), an extremely powerful and wealthy man. He was the son of Charles V's famous chancellor, Pierre d'Orgemont, brother of the Bishop of Paris, and himself Master of the *Chambre des Comptes* and a Canon of Notre-Dame. Apparently he thought himself above reprimand, since he had the Belle Heaulmière installed in one of the houses of the cloister of the cathedral, against all ecclesiastical regulations. Finally, though, in 1416 he became involved in a mysterious plot against the King, was tried by the Chapter of Notre-Dame, and condemned to confiscation of all his property and perpetual prison on "the bread of pain and water of anguish". After being paraded around Paris in a garbage-cart and hearing a sermon on his sins preached in front of the cathedral, he was taken off to the prison of the Bishop of Orléans at Meung (the same one Villon was to see the inside of 45 years later) where he died towards the end of that year.

This must have been quite a blow for the Belle Heaulmière. According to what Villon says, she must have then taken on a pimp who died around 1426. When Villon knew her (before his departure from Paris in 1456) she must have been around eighty, certainly old and decrepit enough to merit the complaints Villon puts in her mouth.

54. In Villon's day, full-time prostitutes were getting quite a run-around from the police, and were being more or less replaced by girls who gained part of their livelihood as shopkeepers (hence the names in this ballade).

55. Most scholars agree that the scatterbrained clerk, Fremin, is a fictitious character, and that Villon did not dictate his *Testament* as he pretends he is doing. Fremin also pops up in lines 779 and 787.

56. For Saint Anthony's fire, see note 31 to *The Legacy*. For the meaning here it's helpful to know that it was also called *le mal des ardents* ("the disease of burning people").

57. Here, a passage from the Decree of Gratian (see Longnon-Foulet, p. 111) is applied to a situation for which it wasn't exactly intended.

58. The word "workman" is best defined by a little ditty from the period:

> If I love my lover
> more than I do my husband,
> it's small wonder:
> he's the finest workman
> in that merry trade
> that's done without a candle.

See also note 79.

59. Either Villon's classical mythology was not too strong, or he is making a joke out of it: Cerberus had only three heads, and Narcissus did not die from the love of a woman, but from his own beauty.

60. Sardana is somewhat of a mystery. Villon might be referring to Sardanapulus, who according to Greek legend was the last king of Assyria and was known for his effeminacy, but this man never conquered Crete.

61. This is a reference to the way peasant women washed (and still wash) their laundry in streams, beating it with a stick.

62. Apparently it was the custom then for wedding guests to pummel each other, saying *"des nopces vous en soubvienne"* ("remember this wedding!"). There is a rather violent account of such proceedings in Rabelais (IV, 14).

63. "Men that ride on brooms" are witches, an occupation not confined to the feminine sex in the Middle Ages.

64. Villon here uses the jargon of dice-players, so I've done the same.

65. Villon's stay in the dank prisons of Meung had probably brought on a lung disease of some sort. Later he tells us that all the hair on his body was falling out (line 1695). *Jacobin* was a somewhat anti-clerical word for a gob of phlegm. Jeanneton here means girls in general.

66. Tacque Thibaud was a favorite of Jean, Duc de Berry, and detested for his exactions and debauched life. Villon here uses his name as an insulting nickname for the Bishop of Orléans, Thibaud d'Auxigny (for whom see biography and note 35 to the *Testament*).

"Cold water" can either refer to the usual prison diet of bread and water, or to a common medieval torture which involved forced drinking of cold water.

"Poire d'angoisse" has a triple meaning: literally it is a specific fruit, the choke-pear, figuratively it means "bitter

fruit", and it also referred to a torture instrument, for a description of which see the note 203 to the Poems in Slang. *Et reliqua* means "and so on".

67. Thibaud d'Auxigny's lieutenant was a certain Pierre Bourgoing. His official was Master Etienne Plaisance (this is why Villon calls him "pleasant"), canon of the church of Saint-Aignan in Orléans and doctor of law. He seems to have been a hard, cruel and somewhat sadistic dispenser of justice. Master Robert was probably the executioner of Orléans. Lombards were the usurers of the period in Paris. This whole stanza, therefore (like the second half of the preceding one), is nothing but sarcasm.

68. For the Bâtard de la Barre (Perrenet Marchand) see note 23 to the *Legacy*. It being a notable fact that too much love-making results in a weakness of the knees, Villon here gives him matting as a support.

69. Moreau was a *rôtisseur* (a man who prepares and sells roast meat), Provins was a pastry-chef and Robin Turgis was the owner of the famous *Pomme de Pin* tavern, for which see *Legacy*, note 18. They were Villon's heirs either in the sense that they had acquired all of his possessions in payment for food and drink, or in the somewhat reverse sense that he still owed them money.

70. For the imaginary clerk, Fremin, see note 55 above.

71. The parable of Lazarus and the rich man is from Luke XVI, 19-31.

72. The Nine Orders are the Nine Choirs of Angels.

73. For Guillaume de Villon see the biography and *Legacy*, line 70.

74. For the *Romance of the Devil's Fart*, Villon's lost early work concerning the student escapade of 1451-2, see the biography.

    For Guy Tabary, one of the crew that robbed the College of Navarre, also see the biography. Villon's referring to him as a "very honest fellow" is probably a wisecrack about Tabary's inability to keep his mouth shut.

75. The Egyptian is Saint Mary of Egypt.

    Theophilus was the hero of a legend very popular in the Middle Ages. To regain his job he made a pact with the devil, but then was redeemed by Our Lady. Its most famous version was a play by the 13th-century poet Rutebeuf called "*Le Miracle de Theophile*".

76. The church described here is undoubtedly that of the Celestines, destroyed in the Revolution. A contemporary of Villon, Guillebert de Metz, describes it thus: "In the Celestines there is a painting of Paradise and Hell, with other nobly executed pictures in a separate choir. Before

the main choir there is an altar painted with the image of Our Lady and masterfully done."

77. Rose, here, is not a girl's name, but rather an epithet for Villon's mistress.

78. *Escu ne targe*, which I have feebly translated "money", has a triple meaning: 1) They both are words for "shield"; 2) they are also both names of coins (the latter a Breton coin) and both reappear in *Testament,* line 1271; 3) in addition *targe* has an erotic meaning which, in the context, is not too difficult to guess.

79. If he ever really existed, Michaud, the Fearless F---er, quickly passed into legend. He is first mentioned in a poem called *Contrefait de Renart* (1328), where the wife of Ysengrin the wolf, annoyed at his apathy, says in effect, "How I'd like to be born all over again, but a man this time. Would I wreak havoc! Why there wouldn't be one woman I'd spare." She ends with these lines:

> Even Michaud, who died of it,
> wasn't such an eager workman as I.

For the word "workman" see note 58 above. As for the tomb Villon mentions at Saint-Satur, it might have existed. Graves with erotic or scatalogical epitaphs were apparently no rarity then.

80. Among Villon's friends, the one most resembling the above-mentioned Michaud is Perrenet Marchand, and sure enough, here he is again. His former appearances were in the *Legacy,* line 177, and the *Testament,* line 764. (See notes 23 and 68).

81. The first two stanzas of this ballade contain an acrostic: FRANÇOIS and then MARTHE. Thus we might interpret the second stanza as meaning, "I would have been better off with Marthe, rather than with 'Rose'". The third stanza has turned some scholars into amateur detectives. They say that if line 962 were to begin *Las, viel seray* (which it doesn't), then this stanza would contain an acrostic reading VJJLLON which would equal VIILLON which would equal VYLLON which would equal VILLON. This seems to be stretching credibility a bit far.

82. For Ythier Marchand, in the preceding stanza, see *Legacy,* note 7. Marchand never did put this poem to music, but whoever did seems to have been a composer of considerable talent. The piece is best performed with voice and two instruments, and it should be remembered that the first verse is repeated in its entirety at the end.

Previous editors, apparently working without the music, seem to have overlooked the fact that this is a standard rondeau. Hence the word *Death,* which has always appeared as the final word of each stanza, actually was the signal for the return of the opening lines.

Qui m'as ma mais-

- - - tres - - se ra - vi

vi - - e   Se

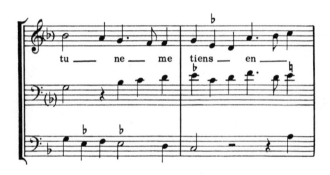

tu ___ ne ___ me   tiens ___ en ___

lan - - - - - gueur.

83. For Jean Cornu see *Legacy*, note 8. Master Pierre Baubignon was an advocate at the Châtelet and seems to have been a tremendous miser involved in endless lawsuits. One of these concerned some gardens which he was ordered to fix up and sell to pay a debt. It is undoubtedly to one of these that Villon refers, and from what he says we gather it had a little ruined house in it. In the next stanza, the paving-stone, hoe-handle and hook which he used as a sign were probably weapons used in nighttime forays, and the gardens and house (so dark that falcons couldn't see) a retreat from the inquiring eye of the authorities.

84. For Pierre de Saint-Amand, whose wife Villon apparently detested, see *Legacy*, note 9. The White Horse and the She-Mule were, of course, house-signs; the meaning of these last three lines is: "To the White Horse which doesn't move (i.e., Saint-Amand who is decrepit and sexually feeble) I give a mare (a woman of passion) in exchange for the She-Mule (his wife who is sterile and frigid); and to said She-Mule I give a red-hot ass (which should be self-explanatory. Cf. "the ass's game" in *Testament*, line 1566) in exchange for the White Horse (her husband).

85. Denis Hesselin was a fiscal judge (an *Élu* was a member of a tribunal in charge of tax litigations), and evidently a man with a certain fondness for liquid refreshment. As we've seen before (note 69), Robin Turgis was the owner of the *Pine-Cone* Tavern; he also worked for the Treasury as a messenger.

86. Concerning Guillaume Charruau's identity the situation is so confused that I won't go into it here. As for Marchand and the sword, see *Legacy*, 81-83 and note 7. Here the pun of the *Legacy* is carried somewhat further, since a *reau* was not only a particular kind of coin, but a *rot* (similarly pronounced) was a belch. The Templars, of course, are the Knights Templars.

87. For Pierre Fournier see *Legacy*, note 20.

88. For the great drinker, Jacques Raguier, see *Legacy*, note 18. *Placques* were Flemish coins of very small worth.

89. For Merbeuf and Louviers see *Legacy*, note 32. Villon here makes short work of any pretensions to nobility they might have had by claiming the only use they would have had for falconry would be to steal birds from Madame Machecoue's poultry shop.

90. Robin Turgis we've already met twice, in lines 774 and and 1017 of the *Testament*. The right to become *échevin* (a city magistrate) was limited to those born in Paris.

Obviously this right was not alienable, which fact somewhat negates the value of the gift.

The southern dialect Villon mentions here is used in the next stanza. I have tried to suggest its flavor by rendering these lines in a dialect of the American south.

91. As stated before (*Legacy*, note 15) little more is known about Jean Raguier than what Villon tells us here. The Twelve were mounted sergeants who formed the personal guard of the Provost of Paris. In addition to the meaning I have in the translation, to give someone a *tallemouse* also meant to give them a punch.

Jean de Bailly, a man with important posts in the Parliament and in the Treasury, lived in a house right next to the Maubué fountain. Thus Raguier, after stuffing himself, would only have had a short walk to partake of a liquid he probably abhorred.

92. The Prince of Fools, the person in charge of organizing various festivities in Paris, was then Guillaume Gueroust. Michault du Four was a tipstaff (constable) of the Châtelet with a number of side-lines (including that of tavern-keeper and butcher), and was one of the men who participated in the inquest on the College of Navarre robbery. The two lines about his jokes and his singing are undoubtedly meant sarcastically.

93. The Two Hundred Twenty were the foot sergeants under the command of the Provost who were in charge of maintaining order, in other words, the municipal police. As one might imagine, they were quite far from being honest, good and gentle. A *cornete* was not only the silk or velvet band worn hanging from the hat, but was also a word for the hemp rope used in hanging. The reason Villon had no dealings with the mounted sergeants was that their jurisdiction was outside Paris.

94. For the infamous Perrenet Marchand see *Legacy*, note 23 and *Testament*, lines 764 and 937. In heraldry the bar sinister is a mark of illegitimacy.

95. Casin Cholet and Jean le Loup are the two colorful citizens described in note 24 of the *Legacy*.

96. *The Woodsmith* was probably the nickname of Jean Mahé, a tipstaff at the Châtelet. We have a record in which he is mentioned as one of the five who tortured the Duke of Nemours in 1476. He is given the ginger because it was then regarded as a strong aphrodisiac. "Tails" and "eels" are colloquialisms for "penis".

97. Jean Riou was a furrier who had been chosen captain of the Hundred Twenty Archers, a kind of volunteer Parisian

militia. Nobody, of course, ever ate wolf meat or used the fur to line a coat.

98. Robinet Trascaille was clerk to Jean le Picart, treasury counsellor to the King and in 1457 was made tax-collector at Château-Thierry. Finally in the year after Villon wrote these lines he was made secretary to the King. He must have gleaned quite a bit of money from these various posts, because Villon's gift of the bowl is pure sarcasm.

99. About Perrot Girart we know no more than Villon tells us here, but what we know about the Abbess of Pourras is extraordinary enough to be recounted in some detail. Pourras, incidentally, was the vulgar name for Port-Royal, the abbey which was later to become so famous through Pascal and Racine. In the 15th century, though, it was not exactly a center of lofty theological discussion.

The abbess then was Huguette du Hamel who was said to be the daughter of the Abbot of Saint-Riquier. She became a nun towards 1439 and abbess of Port-Royal in 1451 or 1455. She then established as attorney for the abbey a certain Master Baudes le Maître; not only were they lovers, but they turned Pourras into a house of revelry probably rarely paralleled in monastic history. Once, for instance, Huguette and Baudes were taking a bath together when she ordered a young nun called Alison to hop into another tub with a cousin of Baudes who was present. Alison, being of a prudish nature, refused, whereupon Huguette had her tossed in, clothes and all. Now that they were wet, she was forced to take off her clothes and thus bring a life of virtue to an abrupt end. Later on it would seem that this Alison was sold by Huguette to her natural father, the abbot of Saint-Riquier. As may be well imagined, this lady acquired a certain notoriety, and the Church started to take a dim view of her doings. After much wrangling they finally made her part company with Baudes, only to have her invest the abbey's money to give the poor fellow a little income. The story ends with them going off together, absconding with the titles and other documents pertaining to the abbey.

100. For the Mendicants, *Filles-Dieu* and Béguines see *Legacy*, note 29. The Turlupins were a sect of heretics. For anyone interested in medieval cooking, here is the recipe for a Jacobin soup: "Take the best cheese one can find, put it on toast and soak it all in beef bouillon. Then put on top good roast plovers or good capons."

101. "Handsome fathers" was a popular name given to monks.

102. Jean de Poullieu was a Doctor of the University of Paris who had been forced to retract what he had said in his sermons against monks. Jean de Meung was one of the authors of the *Roman de la Rose* (for which see note 42) in which he has many unkind words for the hypocrisy of monks. Matheolus was the author of a particularly violent diatribe against the Mendicant Orders. Naturally all of Villon's statements about submitting himself to them are pure irony.

103. Brother Baude was probably the Carmelite monk, Baude de la Mare. It would seem that none of the Parisian Carmelites of Villon's day led particularly saintly lives. Once a group of them was arrested along with some girls disguised as Carmelites, taken to the Châtelet and there divested of clubs and other weapons. At about the same time, a prostitute who was a servant to one of the old monks was chased out of the monastery for having induced several of the younger monks "to commit suspect acts".

No one is sure who De Tusca is, but he might be Jean Turquant, the criminal lieutenant of Paris and the Provost's right-hand man.

Caige vert (undoubtedly a house-sign) might have been a nickname for one of Baude's girl friends, but "cage" also had an erotic meaning which the following ditty by the late 14th-century poet, Deschamps, should make clear. A woman infuriated by her husband's numerous infidelities says—I'll get my revenge:

> By getting a bird
> who'll furnish my cage
> and comfort me.

In addition "arms" had an erotic meaning which should not be too difficult to fathom.

104. "Bee-dung" is Villon's phrase for "wax", so much of which the Sealer has consumed licking it that Villon gives him some pre-spit-upon wax. The squashed thumb is bequeathed him either because when it is flattened out pressing the whole seal down at once would be easier, or because with a crushed thumb it would be impossible to press down a seal at all. Concerning this, commentators line up on either side of the fence and leave the reader to straddle it.

105. The Auditors were the members of the Chambre des Comtes, whose room next to the Palace on the Île-de-la-Cité had an ancient stone ceiling which occasionally let

fall a stone or two, thereby endangering the Auditors and then letting in rain. The High Court near them had a paneled wood ceiling which they must have greatly envied.

Macé d'Orléans was a man (a judge) whom Villon sneeringly treats as a woman.

106. François de la Vacquerie was the Bishop's attorney in charge of pursuing criminal cases pertaining to clerics, and as such a detested man. "Throat piece" is a euphemism for "hangman's noose", and "dubbing" (which consisted of a blow on the shoulder) a euphemism for a beating.

107. Master Jean Laurens was the procurator in charge of investigating the College of Navarre robbery. In addition to his other duties, he seems to have been a dedicated drinker. The Archbishop of Bourges was Jean Coeur, son of the famous Jacques Coeur (see note 47) and therefore extremely wealthy.

108. Master Jean Cotart, who defended Villon in court, is one of the few people Villon mentions with affection. He had just died (9 January 1461), which is why Villon composed the very touching and famous prayer for this drunkard's soul.

109. For the drunkenness of Noah and Lot see Genesis IX, 20 and XX, 30-36. Architriclinus, which in the King James Bible is properly translated as governor or ruler of the feast, was thought to be a proper name in the Middle Ages, that of the husband in the marriage of Cana (John II, 8-9). In any case he was one of the first to taste the water Jesus turned to wine.

110. Jean de Marle and his son, Germain, were both money-changers on the Pont-au-Change. Even though "young" might be another piece of Villonesque sarcasm, it is probably the son that the poet had in mind here. For *écu* and *targe* see note 78; an *ange* was a gold coin, and *angelet* both a coin and a kind of cheese.

111. For the "three poor orphans" see *Legacy*, note 25. The choice of the town of Salins is an additional dig on Villon's part: Salins was a big center of salt-making, a process in which these old codgers had a certain interest. As for line 1280, because Saint Mathurin was the patron saint of mad people, the word *mathurin* (or *mathelin*) had come to designate a madman.

112. Pierre Richier was headmaster of a school for children. The *Donatus* was the standard Latin grammar for the children of the period, but Villon probably also intended a pun on the verb *donner* ("to give"). *Ave salus, tibi decus*

is a parody of a Latin hymn to the Virgin. In order to understand it, one must know that *saluts* and *écus* were both coins, the former of gold. The phrase can then be translated as "Hail, gold saluts, glory to thee, O écus." One could even go one pun further and hear *decus* as *des culs* ("arses") since the pronunciation was almost identical.

113. "Great Credo" was a joking term for long-term credit, a thing these old usurers would have nothing to do with. *Flans*, in addition to meaning "custards", also designated the metal disks used in minting money.

114. Money was usually carried in the belt, and misers were depicted as keeping a tight grip on it so it wouldn't fly away.

115. For the "poor young clerks", the titles and rent, and Guillaume Gueldry see *Legacy*, note 26.

116. The College of the Eighteen Clerks was the oldest in Paris, and in Villon's day had quite a bad reputation. A later inquest termed it *non collegium, sed spelunca latronum* ("not a college, but a den of thieves"). The joke here, though, consists in giving this college's pensions to canons of Notre-Dame, whose job it was to distribute them.

117. A collator was a man who had the right to dispense an ecclesiastical benefice. The reason Villon has never seen their mothers is that the mothers of such old codgers had undoubtedly been dead for years.

118. Michault (or Michel) Culdoe and Charlot Taranne were both among the richest of the Parisian bourgeoisie and both belonged to families of money-changers. In order to understand the gift of boots, one must know that, in addition to being something these two rich men don't need, "to put on the boot" was a euphemism meaning "to have intercourse", as in the following lines from a *Sermon on Marriage*:

> "He suddenly put on his boots,
> and mounted on his horse."

119. For the Lord of Grigny, Philippe Brunel, and Bicêtre, see *Legacy*, note 16. The Tour de Billy on the Right Bank was not only in ruins, but in 1460 had been sequestered by the court pending the outcome of a lawsuit between a man who claimed to have a life lease on it, and the Celestines who claimed it was theirs. In short, a fine gift for the cantankerous old Brunel.

120. For Jean de la Garde see *Legacy*, note 30. Villon knew perfectly well what his name was; his pretended mistake

is a nasty crack, as "Thibaud", and "Jean" as well, were both synonyms of "cuckold".

The Genevoys mentioned here could be either of two men, both attorneys at the Châtelet, Pierre or Etienne Genevoys.

121. For Basanier and Mautaint see *Legacy*, note 19. Nicolas Rosnel was also an examiner at the Châtelet. Jean de Rueil came from a rich family and was a judge at the Châtelet. The spices are to be taken from him partly because judges were often paid with them, and also because his brother was a well-to-do spice merchant.

The "lord devoted to Saint Christopher" is Robert d'Estouteville, for whom also see *Legacy*, note 19. The details about his winning his wife at a tournament are historic fact. At Saumur in 1446, René d'Anjou, King of Sicily, held a *pas d'armes* with forty days of tournaments at which Robert d'Estouteville turned up armed almost like a character in a Sir Walter Scott novel, with a turbaned Moor's head as a crest on his helmet and a horse draped in azure cloth.

122. Since Villon has written this *for* d'Estouteville, it should be read as if he wrote it and addressed it to his wife. Her name, AMBROISE DE LORÉ, appears as an acrostic in the first fourteen lines.

123. Jean and Francois Perdrier, sons of a rich money-changer and bourgeois of Paris, were childhood friends of Villon. The third and fourth lines of this stanza are undoubtedly sarcasm, but what he is referring to in the last four is a mystery.

124. The *Taillevent* was a very famous 15th-century cookbook, and Macquaire was a legendary bad cook (there was possibly some confusion in Villon's mind with Saint Macaire of *The Golden Legend* who had power over demons).

125. Andry Couraud was the attorney in Parliament representing René d'Anjou, and later counsellor for the Treasury to the King of France. In addition he was a neighbor of Villon in Paris, and apparently had been no help in obtaining René d'Anjou's patronage for the poet.

Franc Gontier was the hero of a famous poem by the 14th-century poet and musician Philippe de Vitry. He had become a symbol of the happy, simple peasant, of the "Ah got plenty o' nuttin" school of thought.

The last four lines are a reference to Ecclesiasticus VIII, 1.

126. Sidoine was the mistress of Pontus and heroine of a romance that was popular in the 15th century. Hippocras was a hot wine to which had been added sugar, cinna-

mon, ginger and pepper and which was considered a strong aphrodisiac.

127. For My Lady de Bruyères see the biography. When Villon says "graveyards" he is undoubtedly thinking of the Cemetery of the Innocents which was so famous in medieval Paris, and which he describes late in the *Testament* (lines 1734 and following). Apparently it was a popular place for prostitutes to drum up trade. The Linen Market was run exclusively by women, whose gift for verbiage was probably a good match for that of My Lady de Bruyères.

128. Macrobius was a Roman philosopher and grammarian of the early fifth century. His most famous work is the *Saturnalia*.

129. By Montmartre Villon means the nunnery that was on that hill. It was, as he says, very old and by 1461 the place was in a bad state. The buildings were collapsing and the six remaining nuns were so poor that they had to gain their livelihoods by means not exactly commensurate with their vows. They ran a public tavern, sold wine, and men had free access to the place (the last line of this stanza is meant ironically). Things were to get even worse, though. In 1503 it was found that "the abbess and some of the nuns had given birth, one to two and another to four children, and that one nun was then in labor in the abbess' room and yet another pregnant". Mount Valerian contained a hermitage of Anchorites, and clearly Villon would like the two groups to get together.

130. For "the ass's game" ("intercourse") see note 84.

131. La Grosse Margot whom Villon made so famous was the madame of a house near the cloister of Notre-Dame. Aside from the usual business transacted there, it also seems to have been the scene of a good many brawls in which the police had to intervene, such as one in 1452 involving Villon's friend and evil genius, Regnier de Montigny. The bit about the painting may either be a wry crack about excessive make-up, or a reference to a house-sign with the words *Grosse Margot*. *Brulare bigod* (a Gallicisation of the English "by'r Lord, by God") was one of the oaths by virtue of which the English were known in France in the latter days of the Hundred Years' War as "Bigods" and "Goddamns".

132. This ballade, which gives us an insight into yet another facet of Villon's career, is modeled on a type of poem popular in the 15th century called the *sotte ballade*, in which two hideous lovers squabble, fight, scratch, bite, etc. Far from being a take-off or a literary exercise, this

one is an extraordinary confession of the degradation into which Villon had fallen.

133. Marion the Idol, whose real name was Marion la Dentue, we know about because a clerk named Colin de Thou was dragged into court in 1461 and grilled about the whorehouse she kept and accused of being her pimp. The police could get no information out of him, but fined him anyway and ordered him never to frequent Marion's establishment again.

   To understand the last two lines, one must know that in the Middle Ages there were no street-numbers, but each house had a sign which very often indicated the profession of the inhabitants. Villon says here that if prostitution has become *that* common, what's the use of distinguishing brothels by special signs.

134. This Noël Jolis is probably the same fellow as the Noël in line 662 of the *Testament* who had Villon so badly beaten. Henry is Master Henry Cousin, the hangman of Paris.

135. The Hôtel-Dieu was the big hospital in Paris near the Cathedral of Notre-Dame.

136. In those days barbers not only cut hair, but also did minor surgery, which in Villon's case meant treating wounds and other ailments received in night-time forays. Galerne was quite well known in Paris, and was later to become assistant to the King's master barber. The reason Galerne won't be bothered by next summer's heat is that the pneumonia he'll catch from the ice will kill him off before the winter's over.

137. Colin de Cayeux was one of Villon's companions in the College of Navarre robbery, and, as son of a Parisian locksmith, one of the two who picked the lock of the coffer in which the money was held. After this and another job in the church of the Augustines, he had to leave Paris, and he operated for a while in Normandy. His cleverness with locks not only made him a skilled crook, but also enabled him to break out of almost any jail they put him in. In addition, he was very careful always to wear his clerical habit and not let his tonsure grow in, thereby avoiding the law's secular arm. They finally got him, though, in Senlis, and in spite of the appeal of two bishops, he was condemned by a secular court to be "hung and strangled" on September 26, 1460.

138. The hawking of faked indulgences was one of the principal con-games of the Middle Ages. Chaucer's Pardoner is more or less one of this breed.

139. The Quinze-Vingts were the inmates of a hospital for the blind in Paris. Since they were privileged to beg in the Cemetery of the Innocents on holidays, Villon bequeaths his glasses to help them distinguish the skulls there.

140. The Chambre aux Deniers was the body which controlled and recorded the expenditures of the King's household.

141. The remarks about all these men hating avarice and drying out their bones from overwork· are, of course, sarcastic.

   Saint Dominic is here used as a symbol of the Inquisition (and thereby Villon is implying that it's as important to get yourself absolved by the all-seeing inquisitors as by God). Saint Dominic himself was not an inquisitor, but a man who tried to convert heretics by persuasion. His followers, the Dominicans who founded and organized the Holy Inquisition, seem to have found his methods a bit too sluggish and therefore introduced such innovations as trials without witnesses for the defense, torturing to obtain evidence, etc., etc.

142. For Jacques Cardon see *Legacy*, note 13. "Marionette" and "Open up your door, Guillemette" were probably popular tunes of the day. As for the last line, children in the Middle Ages used to go out in groups to buy mustard and sing ditties which, judging from the samples we have left, were none too clean. In addition, mustard had a second meaning which can be gleaned from these lines about a lover making fun of his lady:

>   En trop de lieux brasses moustarde;
>   Vostre mortier ne vault plus rien.
> (You've ground your mustard in so many places
>   that your mortar is no good any more.)

143. The prison mentioned here is undoubtedly that of Meung which broke Villon's health.

144. This is probably Master Pierre Lomer d'Airaines, a member of the clergy of Notre-Dame, and the one responsible for trying to rid the Île-de-la-Cité of prostitutes in 1456. Ogier the Dane was a legendary hero and great protector of female innocence.

145. Alain Chartier (c.1385-c.1433) was a poet, prose writer and diplomat at the court of Charles VII. Villon is here alluding to a passage from *La Belle Dame sans Merci* in which he leaves sick lovers to make songs, ditties and ballades.

146. Jacques James was the son of a wealthy Parisian architect, Jean James, and owner of a house on Sow Street (hence the pun in the seventh line) and also owner of a bath-

house frequented by prostitutes (which helps to explain the third and fourth and the last two lines). Beyond this, though, this stanza is somewhat of a mystery and no commentator has yet given a satisfactory explanation of what these lines were intended to mean.

147. The Seneschal here might well be Pierre de Brézé, Grand Seneschal of Normandy, one of the finest soldiers and knights of the 15th century. He served Charles VII well, and as a result was imprisoned by Louis XI upon his accession to the throne. As for the line about the blacksmith, it is a variant of an eternal country joke about simple-minded people, like the one Wyndham Lewis recounts about the men of Piddinghoe who shoe magpies and hang ponds out to dry.

148. For the Captain of the Watch, Jean de Harlay, see *Legacy*, note 22. About Philibert and Marquet we know nothing, but just because Villon says they are young and handsome, we can fairly safely assume they were old and ugly. The Provost Marshal was Tristan l'Hermite who, as head of a kind of military police, became rather feared and notorious.

149. This is probably Jean Chappelain, a sergeant of the Twelve along with Jean Raguier and the infamous Bâtard de la Barre. The only thing ecclesiastical about him is his name. A "dry mass" is one without consecration.

150. Jean de Calais was a notary at the Châtelet in charge of the verification of wills. Thus Villon chose the perfect man for the job; the only trouble is that the two had never laid eyes on each other.

151. This line is an allusion to the Christian idea that the only true life is that after death, and therefore means the opposite of what it says.

152. Saint-Avoye was a hospital and chapel run by widows turned nuns. Obviously this was no place to bury a mad-hat poet, except as a joke. Furthermore the chapel was on the second floor, and, as Villon himself points out, the floor could not support a proper tomb.

153. The first two lines of this Rondeau are an almost exact translation of the opening words of the Requiem Mass: *Requiem aeternam dona eis, Domine, et lux perpetua luceat eis.* The shaving of the hair (either part of a judicial ordeal or the result of an illness) and the "harsh justice" are all references to Villon's imprisonment at Meung. The whack on the behind was customary for someone being banished.

154. The "great bell made of glass" is a reference to *La Jacqueline*, the largest bell in Paris and situated in one

of the towers of Notre-Dame. (Bells played a very important role in the life of the Middle Ages, and most of the larger ones had names.) In spite of its enormous size, it was fragile (hence "made of glass") and had to be repaired a number of times and finally recast in 1451. The fifth and sixth lines are a reference to the fact that bells were used to sound alarms. The seventh line can be explained by the belief prevalent in Villon's time that bells could dissipate thunderstorms.

Naturally, all this is another joke. The great bells of Notre-Dame were only rung on important occasions, and it is doubtful that Villon's death would have qualified as such.

155. "Loaves of Saint Stephen's kind" are rocks (Saint Stephen was stoned to death). Because the job of bell-ringer was in Villon's day considered fit only for the poorest, he gives it to two of the richest. Guillaume Volant was a very wealthy merchant and salt speculator. When Louis XI in 1461 made his first entry into Paris as King, Volant was the man chosen to offer the city's homage. Jean de la Garde we've met before (*Legacy*, note 30).

156. As executors Villon chooses first three very powerful men, and then three others of a somewhat different breed.

Martin de Bellefaye was approximately Villon's age, but had risen rapidly to become in 1458 Criminal Lieutenant of the Châtelet, and thus the Provost's (Robert d'Estouteville) right-hand man in the judging of the criminals of France. Guillaume Colombel was an enormously wealthy financier who at one time or another held down a variety of important government posts (King's Secretary, King's Counsellor, etc.). Later on he was to get involved in a scandalous affair in which he brought his wife to trial for adultery, stealing money from him and trying to poison him. She was convicted on the first count and lost her dowry; as for the second it turned out that her husband didn't even give her enough money to buy food; the third count was dropped because of insufficient evidence, but from what we know of his character, it would appear that she was reasonably justified in making the attempt, if indeed she did. Michel Jouvenel was the sixth son of the famous Jean Jouvenel des Ursins. All the children obtained lucrative posts in the church or government, and Michel was no exception. He became bailiff of Troyes (the capital of Champagne famous for its fairs in the later Middle Ages), and received several honorary posts under Louis XI. Through his mother, Michelle de

Vitry, he was a close relative of Thibaud de Vitry, another of Villon's victims (see note 26).

157. Here now are the three men of another breed. We have met them all before: Philippe Brunel in the *Legacy*, note 16, Jacques Raguier in note 18, and Jacques James in the *Testament*, note 146.

158. Of the priest Thomas Tricot, all we know is that he must have been a schoolmate of Villon, as they both received their Master of Arts degrees in 1452. The last two lines contain a double-entendre. "To play tennis" also meant "to make love".

159. Guillaume du Ru was a wholesale wine-dealer and Master of the Wine-Dealers' Guild. He must have been a rich and important man, as the wine business was an important one in the 15th century. Villon chose him to tend the lamps because of a joke current then about the relationship between drinkers and lamps lit for saints:

> O quam sunt beati
> Qui peuvent boire de ceste huile!

> (Oh how blessed are they
> who can drink this oil!)

For Villon's loss of hair see note 153. This combined with the pains in the groin have led some to believe Villon to have been suffering from syphilis (which causes loss of hair in its advanced stages), but what he tells us is not enough to draw any definite conclusions.

160. For the religious orders mentioned here, see *Legacy*, note 29, and *Testament*, note 45. The "lovesick fops" are the dandies of the period, who wore yellowish boots laced as tightly as possible (hence the "without complaining") to make their feet look smaller.

161. This stanza is yet another diatribe against his jailers at Meung.

162. Red is the color of the officiating clergy in the Mass said for Martyrs (in commemoration of the blood they shed). Swearing on one testicle is a double-barreled joke. In the first place it was usual then to swear on some relic, and this one is somewhat sacrilegious; secondly it is a reminder of an old legal joke—*testis unus, testis nullus*—which revolves on the latin word *testis* meaning both "witness" and "testicle".

Notes to the
MISCELLANEOUS POEMS

The order in which these poems are presented is that of the Longnon-Foulet edition, and, to the best of our knowledge, represents that in which they were written. Thus the dullness and occasional banalities of the first poem, and to a lesser extent of the next three, can be attributed to their being early works.

163. This poem is largely inspired by Saint Paul's Epistle to the Romans. Lines 13-14 are a reminiscence of Chapter VIII, 18-25, and lines 31-34 refer to XII, 5 or 18.
164. *Quester*, "to take collections", is a reference to the hawker of indulgences, for which see *Testament*, note 138.
165. See *Misc. Poems* XI, line 15, where Villon explains how one can recognize flies in milk.
166. The Bohemians were the Hussites, followers of the reformer John Huss (1374-1415). After he was burned, they formed a revolutionary movement that had central Europe in considerable turmoil for twenty years. The Church, which considered them heretics, and the Bohemian and German nobility, who were terrified by the democratic character of the movement, made numerous attempts to wipe them out, but all of them were unsuccessful. A settlement was finally reached in 1436.
167. It is at best extremely doubtful that this poem is by Villon, but since it is still included in the Longnon-Foulet edition, and since it is quite a powerful poem, I have included it too. I have, however, omitted giving any footnotes; all the proper names can easily be found with the help of a Bible and a classical dictionary.
168. As with the preceding one, the attribution of this poem is extremely doubtful. It's a charming little piece, but in tone and style it is very unlike the rest of Villon's works.

169. Villon apparently wrote this poem while at Blois as a guest of Charles d'Orléans (see biography). The Duke seems to have enjoyed asking people to compose ballades beginning with the line *Je meurs de seuf auprès de la fontaine* and consisting entirely of contradictions (he himself composed several). We still have fifteen of these poems, and even though Villon's by no means represents him at his best, it is interesting to compare his ballade with the others. (All of them will be found in *Charles d'Orléans, Poésies,* edited by Pierre Champion, 2 vols., Paris, 1923-27, pp. 156-203.)

170. The occasion for which this poem was written has baffled scholars for years. The facts are these: after a marriage that had long been childless, a daughter and heiress, Marie, was born to the Duke d'Orléans in 1457; three years later she paid her first visit to the capital of the duchy, amid great celebration; sometime during this period Villon wrote this bombastic poem of gratitude, saying her birth snatched him from the jaws of death. Did her birth somehow save him from a life of hunger and misery (in which case "death" might be a poetic exaggeration), or did her entry into Orléans bring about his release from prison, as would have been usual on such an occasion (in which case "birth" would be the hyperbole)? The wording of the poem is so rhetorical and vague, and the facts at our command so slim, that it is impossible to decide.

171. This is the famous line from Virgil's fourth Eclogue in which the prospective birth of his patron's child is to bring about a return to the golden era, a statement which many in the Middle Ages took as a prophecy of the birth of Christ.

172. The lily (*fleur de lis*) was the heraldic symbol of the French royal family, of which Charles d'Orléans was a member.

173. This passage is from Psalm 92, verse 4.

174. Both of these passages are from Cato's *Disticha de moribus.*

175. This is a reworking (to fit Villon's meter) of the line from Virgil which appears at the head of the poem.

176. This half tragic, half mocking appeal for help to his disreputable friends was apparently written during Villon's imprisonment at Meung in the summer of 1461 (see biography).

177. The *chaudeau* was a hot soup presented after a wedding to the guests.

178. For pious people Monday, Wednesday, Thursday, Friday and Saturday were fast-days; fasting on the remaining two, therefore, was equivalent to eating virtually nothing.

179. This is undoubtedly a reference to a method of torture commonly used in the prisons of the period which involved enforced drinking of water through a cloth. Lines 14 of the *Testament* and 12 of *Misc. Poems* XVI are probably also references to the same thing.

180. For the occasion on which this request to Jean II, Duke of Bourbon, was written, see the biography.

181. For the *fleur de lis* see note 172.

182. Apparently there are no chestnut trees around Patay, and therefore this is a joke similar to that in *Legacy*, line 124 (see note 13).

183. The word "cross" here has two meanings: first of all that of the wooden or stone crosses so often found by the wayside in the Middle Ages, and secondly that of "money" (because one side of coins had a cross on them). The phrase "true cross" is a fairly blasphemous joke, as obviously what Villon means is not that of Calvary, but hard cash.

184. This poem, so important for an understanding of Villon's mind, has been analyzed by an Italian scholar, Benedetto, in a penetrating and suggestive article called *Il dialogo di Villon col suo cuore* (in *Atti della Reale Accademia delle Scienze di Torino*, t.LXXXVII, 1952-53). I mention this not only because his ideas on Villon are fascinating and original (he by no means limits himself to a narrow exegesis of this one poem), but also because many of my readings and interpretations of this poem were suggested by his article.

185. These flies in milk Villon mentioned once before, in *Misc. Poems*, III, 1.

186. In the Middle Ages people believed that planets influenced the course of lives, and that of Saturn was "evil and melancholy".

187. This is an allusion to the Book of Wisdom, VII, 17-19.

188. This is probably a reference to Arphaxad II, the king of the Medes who was defeated by Nebuchadnezzar.

189. These two lines don't rhyme with the corresponding lines in the rest of the ballade. No one knows if the mistake is Villon's or due to a drowsy copyist.

190. First of all, this line is a joke: Villon identifies Paris as being that town near Pontoise, which is roughly equivalent to referring to New York as that town near Forest Hills. Also Villon is implying that it is too bad he's not from Pontoise (where he would come under the King's

justice) instead of being from Paris (where he is under the jurisdiction of the unpleasant Seigneur de l'Isle-Adam, the new Provost of Paris). For all this and the circumstances under which this poem was written, see the biography.

191. This poem, written when Villon's sentence of death was commuted to that of banishment in January of 1463, is a request for three days' grace in which to say goodby to his relatives and pick up a little money. (See biography.) Even in a situation as tragic as this, Villon can't help from breaking into a bit of buffoonery (the beginning of the third stanza).

192. The rather bombastic tone of this line is mitigated by the knowledge that the King referred to Parliament (and also the University) as "Our daughter".

193. This is a reference to Exodus, XVII, 6.

194. The phrase "joined to the Holy Empire" is baffling. Two solutions have been offered: one that Villon is hyperbolically saying it is "joined to the Heavenly Domain", and the other that he is stating it to be descended from the earlier Holy Roman Emperors such as Charlemagne. Even though I have chosen the second (simply because a choice had to be made), neither is very satisfying in view of line 19.

195. Upon being released from the Châtelet in January of 1463 (see biography) Villon wrote this delightful poem to Etienne Garnier, who was the Gate-Keeper there and at best a dubious character. He had had several scrapes with the law and had been inside that prison once himself.

196. The "sermon" (or "homily") to which Villon refers is his death sentence.

197. Hugues Capet was the founder of the Capetian dynasty of France. A medieval legend claimed he was the son of a Parisian butcher, and thus Villon is saying that if he was of such a family, like the new Criminal Lieutenant of the Châtelet, he would not have undergone the water torture (for which see note 179). He is also, of course, implying that the whole prison administration is nothing but a bunch of butchers.

198. *Pépie* is a bird's disease of the tongue which prohibits them from singing. Clotaire was the name of several Merovingian kings of France, all of whom in Villon's time were, and had been for some time, quite dead indeed.

Notes to the POEMS IN SLANG

The language of these poems is that of the Coquillards, the loosely organized underworld of the 15th century. Like much criminal slang, it was intended, to a certain extent at least, to be a secret language, one that outsiders would not understand. In addition it was spoken four centuries ago, and slang often tends to change more rapidly than ordinary speech. One can see, then, why so many scholars have thrown up their hands in despair over these poems.

One small glimmer of light was brought to bear on them, though, when in the 19th century a document concerning the Coquillards was discovered in Dijon. It appears that in 1455 a group of them who had been terrorizing the town were rounded up in a whorehouse they had been using as headquarters and taken off to be questioned by the police. Two of them were finally persuaded to talk: the youngest (on promise of release) and a barber whose shop was frequented by members of the group. Their testimony, which is the substance of the above-mentioned document, is of great interest not only because it gives a lot of names of Coquillards (it's from this that we know Regnier de Montigny and possibly also Colin de Cayeux to have been members), but also because it gives many translations of slang terms.

Naturally this was a great help and gave scholars at least some solid ground on which to tread. Unfortunately, though, only a small part of the slang terms Villon uses in these poems is found in that document. The remainder of his language varies from being reasonably intelligible to utterly impenetrable.

For anyone interested in making further investigations into these fascinating but frustrating poems, there are two principal books that have been written on them:

L. Sainéan, *Les Sources de l'argot ancien*, 2 vols., Paris, 1912. A part of the first volume is devoted to an edition and analysis of these poems by Pierre Champion. Even though he limits himself to interpreting only what is reasonably certain (thereby leaving much unexplained), this is the classic work on the subject.

A. Ziwès & A. de Bercy, *Le Jargon de Maître François Villon*. This work has many faults, but it boldly tackles every problem and offers many interesting suggestions.

In translating these poems, because of the many and sometimes insurmountable problems involved, I have occasionally sacrificed exact meaning to flavor or tone; often, too, the rendering I have chosen is purely conjectural. Such an approach is unavoidable in an area where the terrain is so slippery.

199. Chopping off the ears was the usual punishment of thieves, and more specifically, for purse-snatchers.

200. For Colin de Cayeux see the *Testament*, note 137.

201. This is a reference to the fact that a church in the Middle Ages was a place of sanctuary. In theory at least, the police could not enter one to arrest a person who had taken refuge there, no matter what his crime had been.

202. For Regnier de Montigny, see the *Legacy*, note 14.

203. This is probably a reference to the *poire d'angoisse* ("choke-pear"), a torture instrument that was stuck in the mouth, and then expanded by means of a key so that it could no longer be extricated.

204. This Ostac is probably the same as the de Tusca in line 1194 of the *Testament* (see note 103).

205. "La soe" seems to be a reference to the Pig Market in Paris, which is where counterfeiters were boiled in oil (this was the usual punishment for that crime). The hooks were used to drag them back into the pot when they tried to clamber out.

BIBLIOGRAPHY

For anyone interested in doing more reading on Villon, I will list the few books that are absolutely essential among the veritable jungle of printed matter that has grown up around the poet and his works.

Villon scholarship was founded by Auguste Longnon. His two books, *Étude biographique sur François Villon*, Paris, 1877, and *Oeuvres complètes de François Villon*, Paris, 1892, although now perhaps a bit dated, were the foundation stones for all subsequent research. Since then, the important books are:

EDITIONS

A. Longnon & L. Foulet, *François Villon, Oeuvres*, Paris, 4th edition, 1932. Published in a series called *Les Classiques Français du Moyen Age*, this edition, based on Longnon's of 1892, but having undergone successive improvements, is the classic edition of the text. It is inexpensive and still available.

L. Thuasne, *François Villon, Oeuvres*, 3 vols., Paris, 1923. This is an edition with a voluminous commentary indispensable for studying the text.

A. Burger, *Lexique de la langue de Villon*, Geneva-Paris, 1957. This, a complete dictionary of Villon's works, is not only invaluable, but is the first major step in Villon scholarship in twenty years.

BIOGRAPHIES

P. Champion, *François Villon, sa vie et son temps*, 2 vols., Paris, 1913. 2nd edition, 1933. This, the classic work on Villon's life, is not only a mine of information about the poet and his friends, but also about contemporary Parisian life.

BIBLIOGRAPHY

D. B. Wyndham Lewis, *François Villon, a Documented Survey,* New York, 1928 (and since reprinted). By far the best thing in English on the subject of Villon.

This list does not include books on the *Jargon,* which are a category apart. For these, see the above note to the Poems in Slang.

A complete list of all the writings on Villon (through 1953) can be found in R. Bossuat, *Manuel bibliographique de la littérature française du moyen âge,* Melun, 1952, and a supplement, Paris, 1955.

INDEX OF FIRST LINES

(L=Legacy; T=Testament; MP=Miscellaneous Poems;
S=Poems in Slang)

INDEX OF TITLES

(To make this list more useful to the reader, the titles are, for the most part, given in their more familiar forms.)